Samantha Collett ... property auction
success; she started in 2004 with £15k and within three

Award (West Midlands) 2010.

Other titles from How To Books

THE SMALL BUSINESS START-UP WORKBOOK
Cheryl D. Rickman

THE EASY eBAY BUSINESS GUIDE
Cathy Hayes

SETTING UP AND RUNNING A LIMITED COMPANY
Robert Browning

WRITE YOUR OWN BUSINESS PLAN
Paul Hetherington

A ONE PERSON BUSINESS
Clive Morton

How To Buy Property At Auction

Samantha Collett

howtobooks

Constable & Robinson Ltd
55-56 Russell Square
London WC1B 4HP
www.constablerobinson.com

First published in the UK by How To Books,
an imprint of Constable & Robinson Ltd., 2014

A copy of the British Library Cataloguing in Publication
Data is available from the British Library

ISBN 978-1-84528-523-4 (paperback)
ISBN 978-1-84528-528-9 (ebook)
.
Printed and bound in the UK

1 3 5 7 9 10 8 6 4 2

Contents

Preface

I probably shouldn't start by confessing my addiction to property auctions . . . . but I will! And I hope *you* too will soon experience the joy of buying property at auction.

Property auctions are magical.

They are addictive.

They are compelling.

They are the most wonderful way to buy property.

Auctions offer a whole new property adventure – and it is a journey which is fast-paced, action-packed, fun – and, if you do your sums right, incredibly lucrative.

I have been buying property at auction for ten years – and I love it. In that time I have bought countless properties at auction in every shape and size: from tiny studio flats to commercial premises to wrecks and even a chapel. Along the way I have made money, made mistakes – and I learned from them all.

And now is the time for me to share my experiences. While property auctions are my first love, my second love is talking about property auctions: which is why I wrote this guide. Buying property at auction is awesome – however, you do need to know a few ground rules and understand the process before you leap in.

How to Buy Property at Auction will guide you through the essential steps you need to successfully bid and win property at auction. I've packed the guide full of key tips, insights, checklists, case studies and pitfalls to watch out for. And I've tried to write it in an easy-to-read style so that you don't get bamboozled.

So I'm hoping you're ready for your property auction adventure . . . and I will see you in the auction rooms very soon.

Acknowledgements

'If you enjoy what you do, you will never work another day in your life.'

(Confucius)

This pretty much sums up my life as a property investor – and it is a most enjoyable life!

But no enjoyable life can be created alone.

From the first moment I decided on property investment as a career choice, Dimitris has supported and encouraged me all the way, and his unwavering belief in me has been astonishing. And so the same is true with this book. Dimitris has backed me from the start and urged me to make time and space for this project – with the same importance as if it had been a property development. I am eternally grateful for his continued support, never-ending patience and ability to put up with my mad ideas.

I am incredibly fortunate to have a supportive family who always push me to try more, to be more and achieve more. Their belief in me keeps me strong. Thanks Mum and Kevin – and Dad I know you would have been proud of me.

I am also blessed to have the most wonderful friends who continue to amaze me with their help and assistance. I would like to thank them all for their kind words and encouragement, and special thanks are due to Nick Dare, James Dearsley, Jo Johnson, Jo King, Nick Parkin and Ruth

Partlett, whose dedication to helping me and encouraging me ensured this book became a reality.

Without the guidance of Anita Rattigan, this whole book idea would never have come to fruition. From the outset, she believed in me and pushed me further than I had ever thought was possible for me as a writer.

I also have to say thanks to all my wonderful blog readers who have been a great source of inspiration for me and a bedrock of support.

I owe a massive debt of gratitude – for their valuable contributions and insights – to Andrew Binstock, Director & Auctioneer at Auction House London; Guy Charrison FRICS FNAVA FNAEA FARLA FRSA Chartered Surveyor and 2011 to 2013 President of the National Association of Valuers and Auctioneers; Michael John Hayward, solicitor. Without them sharing their professional expertise this book would not have been half the book it is!

Over the years I have been fortunate to work and talk with so many people in the property industry. I would like to take this opportunity to say thank you to everyone for sharing your stories, your experiences and your learnings with me. Without you, my learning curve would have been much steeper – and my mistakes much more expensive.

And to all the auctioneers whose auctions I have ever attended: thank you for creating such a fun, fulfilling and thrilling way to buy property.

CHAPTER 1

The Not So Secret World of Property Auctions

'I used to think property auctions were for "other" people and not for the likes of me . . . then I went to an auction and there were so many normal people . . . just like every day Joes . . . there were lots of people like me!'

(Ken, auction property buyer)

You'd never guess, but every day, properties are being sold under the hammer. All across the country thousands and thousands of properties are bought and sold at auction. It's a multi-billion pound business. From stately homes to war bunkers, repossessions to roads, everywhere you look properties are being snapped up by savvy investors, developers and people just like you.

It's just a case of knowing where to look.

To the uninitiated, the world of property auctions can seem a different world. A crazy world where any sort of property, anywhere, can be bought and sold. It's true. And that is what makes property auctions so amazing.

You don't have to be crazy to buy at auction, but you do need to be ready to start a new property adventure. You need to be prepared for cut-price bargains. You need to be equipped with a new set of rules. You need to be organised, open-minded and ready for anything; to act fast and think quick. You need to have courage, confidence and some cash and be prepared to enter a whole new world of buying property – and making money.

So if you're ready for your new property adventure, let's get started.

A very British love affair

'An Englishman's home is his castle.'
(Proverb)

In the UK we love our homes. We are passionate about property: from owning our own home to buying houses for other people to make their homes in. We are driven by some kind of primordial force which makes us love, lust and lose all control when it comes to property. Don't ever get between a Brit and their building – war will erupt.

Property investment is big business: there are an estimated 1.4 million private landlords in the UK and the figure is growing all the time. Buy-to-let is huge, and it's because people love property; people need property. People need somewhere to live, somewhere to love and somewhere to call home. And if you invest in an asset class that is so basic, so essential and so cherished, it's not hard to understand why wanting to invest in property is a national obsession.

Property is real. Property can be touched. It gives power to the people. Stocks and shares, gilts and bonds exist in a fairy-tale land – bits of paper and electronic data which are controlled and sold by rich bankers ensconced in their swanky offices. Property can be visited and valued, improved and extended, rented and sold. Property can be passed on, made personal, impersonal, knocked down and rebuilt. Property can be made to be all things to all people, or some things to some people, but in short: property is about people.

And that is why we love it.

The property auction adventure

Now, just imagine being able to buy property quicker, easier and maybe even cheaper. . . .

You'd be there.

You'd be there in a shot.

If only you knew where to go . . . which is why you have bought this guide!

You too want to join the ranks of successful property auction buyers. You too want the excitement, thrill and experience of bidding to buy at auction. You too want the chance to bag a bargain, to modernise the unmodernised, to love the unloved and to make a bit of money along the way.

You too want to start a whole new property adventure.

And you are welcome to join us.

How to use this guide

Property auctions offer fantastic opportunities for you to make a whole heap of cash, but can also lose you a bucket-load. Buying property at auction can be a sure-fire route to success – but only if prudence, due diligence and vision are made the masters. It may sound complicated, but there are simple steps to auction success – follow them and you too will be regaling the legendary tales of buying property at auction.

In this guide we will look at:

- Why people buy property at auction.

- What happens behind the scenes of an auction house.

- How to find and view auction property and turn 'detective'.

- How to prepare for auction success including organising surveys, legal advice and finance.

- How to research the property market, cost the works and calculate the bid price.
- What to expect on auction day and how to bid.
- What to do once you've won your lot . . . and how to cope if you get outbid.
- Real auction room stories of profit and loss to inspire and caution.
- Simple steps and top tips to auction success.

Throughout the journey I have included real case studies, insights, anecdotes and tips to bring the adventure to life. At the end of each chapter there is a summary of the key learnings and additional insights, tips and watch points.

Anybody can buy property at auction – whether you're a first-time buyer, looking for a new challenge after redundancy, or just wanting to make some extra money – and soon it could be you.

Be excited. Be brave. But be cautious, too.

CASE STUDY: A FIRST-TIME AUCTION BUYER

'My boyfriend and I had been looking to buy our first house for some time. We had managed to raise the deposit and then the financial crisis hit; it was really hard trying to get a mortgage. Luckily, we both had secure jobs and were not looking to borrow too much, so we managed to find a bank that would still lend to us. The only problem we did have was the prices of the properties we wanted to buy were still too high and no vendors seemed willing to negotiate. Then one day we saw a property online. We hadn't realised it was an auction property and didn't really know what that meant so we went along to the viewing anyway. It needed a lot of work, but we thought it had potential. We spoke to our bank and found a solicitor who checked everything for us before the auction.

The whole experience was really nail-biting – although very exciting as well! We were so happy when we managed to buy our house at just less than our final bid price. We did have to do everything very quick and that was pretty stressful at times . . . We reckon we saved at least 20 per cent buying at auction rather than through an estate agent, which meant we had more money to improve the property and really make it ours.' (Brian, first-time auction buyer)

CASE STUDY: STARTING YOUR OWN BUSINESS

'I had been working at the local café for about five years when the owner had to sell due to ill health. I didn't have the funds available to buy the business and wasn't sure what I was going to do next. There were not many jobs available and I found it difficult to get excited about my options. I had always thought about running my own café and making my own cakes, but I didn't think I had the money to make a go of it. Then one day, my husband and I were out shopping in a neighbouring town and I saw a building which I thought would make an ideal café. I phoned up the agents and found out it was going to auction the next month. We went and viewed and we fell in love. It would be perfect for me as my own little café! That night my husband and I drew up all the business plans and calculated how we could make it work. We spoke to a mortgage broker about releasing equity from our own house to buy the building. We had a tight budget and a strict limit, but we knew we were making the right decision to start our own business. I was so nervous on auction day – my hand was shaking as I bid on the property. I couldn't believe it when we won it. The café has been hard work, but we look set to make a profit and I am so pleased to now have my own business and my own place after buying at auction.' (Helen, small business owner)

Secret language of property auctions

Everywhere in the world there is jargon to be understood and the world of property auctions is no different. I have tried to use plain English wherever possible, but sometimes I need to use jargon just because that is the only available term.

Here is a list of the key terms which you should familiarise yourself with so that you can get the most out of this guide:

- Lot: this means the property (or land, etc.) which is being sold. The term 'lot' refers to the lot number in the catalogue. Very often, when you are talking with the auctioneers, they may not know the property address, but instead will know the lot number. You can think of it rather like the catalogue number which you would use in Argos when you want to order an item.

- Guide price: this is exactly as it says – it is a *guide price* to give people an idea of what they might expect to pay for a property. It is not a minimum nor a maximum, it is purely a guide. Guide prices can be set quite low to attract early interest in a property. However, guide prices are usually set within 5–10 per cent of the reserve price.

- Reserve price: this is the lowest price that the seller is willing to accept for the property. Sometimes vendors are willing to disclose the reserve prior to auction and the auction catalogue entry will state 'Disclosed reserve £X'; however, usually vendors do not disclose the reserve until after auction and if the property did not sell. Occasionally, properties are sold with no reserve.

- Stock: this refers to the properties that are for sale in an auction catalogue. Think of the 'stock' of an auction house as being similar to the stock a supermarket might carry. Stock is the available property an auction house has listed for sale. Auction houses tend to specialise and become known for their stock – for instance, one auction house may be known for selling residential lots in London whereas another may be known for selling commercial properties in Wales.

- Bid: this means you are making a proposal to purchase the property. A bid is an official offer and can be both verbal and non-verbal (such as raising your hand in the auction room). Once a bid is made and accepted it becomes legal and binding.

CHAPTER 2
Why Buy a Property at Auction?

'Property auctions are addictive, you never know what you are going to find. I turn up and regularly buy properties which I never intended buying!'

(David, regular auction buyer)

Many people are attracted to the idea of buying property at auction. They are turned on by the cut and thrust of the auction room, plus the chance to bag a bargain. Buying a property at auction has increasingly become a popular way to buy property.

Unlike properties sold with an estate agent, auction properties hold a mystical quality that casts a dreamlike spell on potential buyers. And it must be magic – because nowhere else do you find perfectly sane, logical people willing to part with hundreds of thousands of pounds for properties they have never even seen. Buying 'blind' is a regular occurrence at property auctions, but this is *not* a recommended practice.

The truth is, buying a property at auction is an exhilarating experience from start to finish – not least because of the chance of finding undiscovered treasure or a unique opportunity that nobody else has seen. Whether or not black magic is at work in the auction room is a moot point, but, without a doubt, buying a property at auction is an experience you will never forget – and hopefully, as for most successful auction buyers, one that you will want to repeat time and time again.

In this chapter, we will look at the main reasons why people buy property at auction:

- Variety

- Price

- Speed

- Certainty

- Transparency

From reading this chapter you will gain an understanding of the reasons why people buy property at auction.

Property auctions offer variety

People frequently wonder what sort of properties are on offer at auction – in a nutshell it's anything and everything!

Auctions offer an enormous variety of properties for sale: from repossessed houses to building plots, business premises to castles and everything in between. Auctions offer a massive selection of properties for sale which you won't often find in an estate agent's window.

The following types of property will usually be found in a property auction catalogue:

- Repossessed property, unmodernised property, probate sales

- Former sewerage works, water pumping stations, old railway land, war bunkers

- Car parks, MOT centres, garages, petrol stations and roads

- Stately homes, manors, halls, castles and moats

- Sea forts, beaches, marinas, piers and beach huts

- Chapels, churches and graveyards

- Forests, lakes, fisheries and disused quarries

- Industrial buildings: potteries, warehouses, factories, offices, advertising hoardings

- Former council buildings: surgeries, libraries, police stations, job centres, public toilets

- Leisure buildings: swimming pools, bingo halls, theatres, hotels and guest houses

- Land of all shapes and sizes (with and without planning permission)

- Supermarkets, banks, shops, cafés, pubs and restaurants

- Investment property: property which is already rented to a tenant

- Job lots of property: from blocks of flats to actual streets of houses.

Examples of the variety of property available at auction.

The incredible choice of properties available makes the auction house a very attractive place to buy. In fact, it is the sheer variety of properties and opportunities available at auction that attracts many buyers to the sale room in search of something 'a bit different'.

Oddly enough, what is termed an 'unusual' property for an estate agent is most likely to be 'usual' property in the auction room. For example, repossessed properties and houses requiring modernisation are scarce finds with an estate agent and are often sought-after opportunities which can provoke bidding wars; however, in an auction these same types of properties are ten a penny! At an auction it would be unusual to find a property that *didn't* need work or wasn't repossessed.

Moreover, when was the last time you saw an estate agent selling an electricity sub-station as an investment opportunity, or maybe a car park . . . or even a Tesco super-market? Property auctions offer a massive variety of different opportunities to suit every pocket and every person. And the extensive choice available means the world literally is your oyster in terms of what sort of property you want to buy . . . and even what sort of lifestyle you want to lead.

How about this property for something 'a bit different'?

CASE STUDY: CASTLE COVE BEACH – A NEW LIFESTYLE OPPORTUNITY?

Castle Cove. (Source: Symonds & Sampson Auctioneers, 2011)

A sandy beach overlooking Portland's 2012 Olympic Harbour with lifestyle business opportunity.

An exciting opportunity to acquire a sandy beach with stun-ning panoramic views over Portland Harbour, which will host the 2012 Olympic sailing events. The current owners run a successful licensed refreshment business from the kiosk on site, which has planning permission until November 2015 and is currently connected to mains water and electric. There is also a timber-clad store with space for an eco-toilet (not fitted) which has been granted planning permission until 31 May 2012 along with planning permission for the erection of 8 beach chalets/changing cubicles. The beach forms part of the World Heritage Jurassic Coastline. Castle Cove Sailing Club is within a short walk, as is Sandsfoot Castle. The town centre, along with the picturesque inner harbour, is situated within 1.5 miles.

(Symonds & Sampson Auctioneers, 2011)

TIP

Auctions are well known for the variety of properties they sell, but you can also find more typical homes being sold.

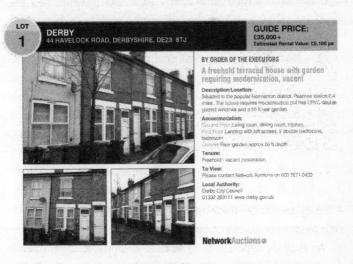

Catalogue entry showing a cheap auction lot.
(Source: Network Auctions, 2013)

Buying a Bargain at Auction

Everybody loves the chance to pick up a bargain – and buying a bargain property has got to be the British dream. Media reports of cheap auction buys have fuelled the excitement of the potential savings to be had (plus the money to be made) from buying property at auction. If you do your homework right, there are plenty of property bargains to be bought.

Properties sold at auction are regularly offered much more cheaply than you would find with an estate agent. How much cheaper often depends on the location, works required and the circumstances of the sale. Typically, auction sale prices will be around 15–35 per cent cheaper than the equivalent price with an estate agent. But what really excites the auction-buying crowd is the possibility of buying the property for even less . . . and it is the 'come-and-buy-me' guide price which will tempt many people into the auction room for the chance of a really *extreme* bargain – a property at up to 60 per cent less than the open market value.

Of course, these sorts of extreme property bargains are scarce – but they do happen and they happen often enough to be the stuff of auction house legend. They are the property 'pots of gold' that everybody dreams they will chance upon – the overlooked lot, the diamond in the rough that nobody else but *you* saw the potential in. And it is this thrill of discovering a potential gold mine of a property that really motivates most auction buyers. The joy of unearthing a bargain from a building is an incredible feeling – and one which could potentially put thousands of pounds in your pocket.

TIP

Do not assume auction property is always cheap, or cheaper than estate agents, just because it is being sold at auction.

LOT 4

LONDON
FLAT 5, 51 EARLHAM GROVE, FOREST GATE, E7 9AN

GUIDE PRICE:
£69,000+
Current Rental Value: £6396 pa

BY ORDER OF CORPORATE CLIENTS

A top floor studio flat subject to a protected tenancy

Description/Location:
Situated in a tree lined street close to Forest Gate station (0.3 miles) and Wanstead tube (0.5 miles). We are advised the tenancy began on 5 January 1995 and the current rent is £123 per week.

Accommodation:
Ground Floor: Communal front door, stairs to 2nd floor
Second Floor: Front door to hallway, bed sitting room, kitchen, shower room.

Tenure:
Leasehold - Lease 125 years from 18 December 2006

To View:
Please contact Network Auctions on 020 7871 0420

Local Authority:
London Borough of Newham
020 8430 2000 www.newham.gov.uk

NetworkAuctions

LOT 28

STEVENAGE
SITE ADJACENT TO GRINDERS END AND A1M, GRAVELEY, HERTFORDSHIRE, SG4 7WH

GUIDE PRICE:
NO RESERVE

BY ORDER OF THE HIGHWAYS AGENCY

A freehold site of 1,845 acres, vacant

Description/Location:
This wooded site lies to the north of Graveley Park and adjacent to the A1M. Speculative future uses include leisure and development subject to planning.

Tenure:
Freehold - vacant possession

To View:
Please contact Elliott Network Auctions on 020 7871 0420

Local Authority:
North Hertfordshire District Council
To bid 01908 www.north-herts.gov.uk

Elliott
NetworkAuctions SMITHSGORE

CASE STUDY: THE (UN)WANTED BLACKPOOL HOTEL

It was close to the end of a long auction day. Mr Singh had travelled over 200 miles to attend the property auction in London but had been outbid on the lot that he had come for. The auction room was now almost empty with just a few stragglers hanging around, leafing through the auction catalogue to see what else would be sold.

The auctioneer called out the next lot – a hotel in Blackpool. Nobody in the room paid any attention. The auctioneer continued trying to drum up interest in the lot by lowering the opening price – he'd started at £100,000 and had now reduced the initial asking bid to just £65,000. Mr Singh looked at the details in the auction catalogue and saw it was a sizeable property – he had never seen the property before, nor had he even been to Blackpool – but £65,000 sounded a good deal. He put his hand in the air and bid. The auctioneer accepted his bid and called for more potential people to try to increase the price. But nobody stirred. Nobody was interested.

Mr Singh bought the hotel in Blackpool for £65,000 on his maiden bid. He was rather surprised that he had bought the property on just one bid – and instantly regretted his foolhardy actions at auction. However, his bid had been accepted, the gavel had come down, and now he had bought a hotel in Blackpool.

Mr Singh started doing research on his new purchase and the area and soon felt even more unsettled by the purchase he had made – he felt he had made a mistake and bought 'a dog' (a bad property deal).

He was very surprised when just forty-eight hours after the auction sale he received a call from the auction house who had been contacted by an interested party who wanted to buy the hotel in Blackpool from him. In fact, they were so keen to buy the property that Mr Singh could sell on the property immediately to the next party without his even needing to complete on the purchase. The interested party would actually take over the sale and Mr Singh would benefit from the sale price they were willing to pay him for the hotel.

The price they were willing to pay for this supposed 'dog' of a deal? £250,000!

Needless to say Mr Singh accepted on the spot and within twenty-eight days the money was in his bank account – all £185,000 profit – and he hadn't even needed to go to Blackpool!

Auction properties offer you a 'speedy deal'

'Twenty-eight Days Later' may be the title of a British horror movie – but it's also the name of the game when it comes to completing a sale at auction!

Buying a property at auction is much quicker than the usual route of buying with an estate agent. With an estate agent, the process of buying a property typically takes twelve to sixteen weeks from the date of offer acceptance through to actual sale completion. When buying a property at auction, the process typically takes twenty-eight days from the date of auction (the day you have your offer accepted and the sale exchanges) through to the actual sale completion.

Auction properties are bought and sold according to strict time deadlines set out in the legal contract. Unlike buying with an estate agent where everybody works to a target date, in the property auction world the completion deadline is time-critical and legally binding. Most auction contracts will stipulate a sales completion date of twenty-eight days later – which means you will become the new owner of the property twenty-eight days after the auction!

There are also some instances where you will become the new owner even more quickly – for example, if the property has been repossessed, it is quite common for the lender to request a sales completion date just fourteen days later.

Buying property at auction gives you the ability to speed up the process and within days become the new owner – but it also means you need to be prepared. The preparation process prior to auction will be covered in detail later in the book.

CASE STUDY: TIME WAS RUNNING OUT!

'The lease was coming to an end on the office which we had been renting for three years. We liked the building, but knew the landlord was going to increase the rent considerably due to improvements we had made. We were keen to take advantage of the discounted commercial properties which were being sold at auction – but we had to be quick – the lease was running out on our current premises and we needed to move the business quickly. Buying our new office building at auction allowed us to become the new owners within just days of attending the auction which was great news for us – and saved us a fortune!' (Paul, business owner)

TIP

Auction property sales complete faster than private treaty sales. However, preparation and planning can make this possible within the timeframe.

Buying property at auction is a 'done deal'

'The beauty of buying and selling at auction is actually the knowledge you have bought or sold the property. There's no messing about!'
(Andrew Binstock, Auction House London)

'Going once . . . Going twice . . . Going for the third and final time' . . . BANG! The gavel falls . . . and with that simple action you have bought a property!

What most people are unaware of is that at auction the actual moment of contract (when you have committed to purchase the property) is the moment at which the auctioneer bangs down his gavel. The signing of the contract after this moment records the 'memorandum of the contract' – and the price which you have agreed to buy at. But the actual contract is the falling of the hammer on the highest bid.

It is this unique feature of auction law that has spawned a multitude of stories and urban myths around 'scratching your nose and buying a house'! Of course, while it is very easy to bid and buy a property at auction, it has to be said that the auctioneer is well trained and very adept at understanding the difference between a scratch and a bid!

The critical feature to remember when buying a property at auction is that, unlike with an estate agent, once your offer has been accepted the 'deal is done'. There is no scope for gazumping, gazundering or any other gaz-itis: once you've bid and won the property at auction – it's yours!

This certainty of sale is hugely attractive to people who want to know that the house they are buying is the house they are buying. All too often, when buying property with an estate agent, the whole process feels very fragile. Until the day of exchange people are on tenterhooks with regards to the chain above and below. They feel anxious about being asked for more money for the property they are buying, or being offered less for the property they are selling – and even (as happens rather too often) sellers deciding they no longer want to sell and withdrawing their property from the market.

When buying a property at auction – once bought, it's bought. There's no ifs, buts, or maybes – you are soon to be the proud new owner.

CASE STUDY: IAN'S STORY

Rewind a few weeks, and the English property system had just failed us for the third time. Our modest three-bedroom semi had been sold back in August for a price we'd felt lucky to achieve in the current climate. On the day we were meant to exchange contracts on our sale and the purchase of a delightful detached cottage, the chocolate in the chocolate box house started melting. The present owners had underpinned the property of our dreams themselves and not told the insurance company, meaning the deal could not go ahead. So, after committing over £2,000 of our hard-earned cash into it, we had to walk away. Boxes were packed, removal men were booked and the post had already been redirected. Worst of all, we had to move in with relatives, much to my wife's dismay . . .

We retreated back to Rightmove and thought no more of it. When yet another property we wanted to buy fell through, my wife (the reliable, hard-working, organised one) decided that I (the creative, slightly dreamy yet courageous one) might as well go along to the auction just for the experience . . .

Lot 9 was next. The auctioneer took the price down from over £600,000, until someone bid in at £400,000. The price quickly rose, and then came to a sudden halt, at below our maximum price. I had one of those slow-motion moments with the sudden realisation that the next couple of seconds could define my entire life, the realisation that this could be either the best or worst decision I ever make . . . and I bid.

Next followed silence, save for the palpitations of my thumping heartbeat as hundreds of pairs of eyes turned to see who the little upshot was that thinks he can pay that much for a house in this age of austerity. 'Going, going gone. Sold, to the gentlemen on my left!' I honestly couldn't tell you what happened next, but evidently I'd just bought a dream house for about the price of an average London home . . . If you want something enough and fate agrees, pretty much anything is possible. For whom the hammer falls, it falls for thee. ('For Whom the Hammer Falls: How an Auction Changed my Life', Ian Wilson, Huffington Post, blog, 2011)

The auction room offers a transparent buying process

'People like the transparent, open and shut case of buying property at auction. The private treaty equivalent of auction is 'Best and Final Bids', but it always seems to somehow feel tainted and not quite right. The person who was successful feels like they have paid too much and the person who didn't get the property feels like the winning buyer was in some way helped.'

(Guy Charrison, Network Auctions)

Buying property with an estate agent can sometimes feel rather like a cloak-and-dagger affair – offers accepted on a property are shrouded in secrecy and the agent is unable to disclose anything about the price being offered for the property. This is in contrast to buying property at auction where the price being offered is open and visible for all to see.

At a property auction everybody can see what everybody else is bidding and the price they are prepared to pay. The transparency and openness is frankly sometimes infuriating, however, the transparency of the process is one of the greatest strengths of buying at auction.

In the auction room, you can see for yourself whom you are bidding against, you can see how much they are bidding and you can see how many people are bidding. In fact, in the auction room you really can see the *whites of the eyes* of all of your competitors!

It is this transparent process of bidding that is a key attraction for many buyers. Rather than trying to second-guess what the other interested party may offer for a property, they will be present at the auction room and will openly bid in front of you. The price they are willing to pay is there for all and sundry to see.

This makes auction a very open and clear way of buying property and of establishing its value. Unlike buying property with an estate agent, where the value is decided by the agent and/or the vendor, in the auction room the value of the property is determined by the bidders in the room. While there is a guide price and a reserve price, ultimately it is the buyers in the room who decide the final value of a property and the price they are willing to pay. Guide prices are indicative values of a property but they are not the final price. The final price is the price someone is willing to pay for the property on that day at auction.

> 'Auction gives a fair price to a property and it is the market which chooses the price . . . The estate agent model is typically that an agent is chosen for the highest price valued and then over time if the property does not sell the value gets decreased. With auction it is the bidders who make the price. '
>
> (Andrew Binstock, Auction House London)

Many auction buyers feel the transparency of auction gives them more control in the buying process. At auction you have full knowledge of the other interested parties and their bids – this enables you to make a clear decision on the price you are paying, as opposed to buying with an estate agent where offers are kept secret and are not disclosed.

Auctioneer Insight

As a method of sale auctions are the most transparent way to buy property. All of the information is available upfront and you can make an informed decision. When buying private treaty this information is usually found out much later in the process when considerable time and monies have been committed. Buying property at auction enables you to get all of the information upfront; so you know what you're buying – rather than finding out later down the line. (Guy Charrison, Network Auctions)

Insider Insight

Many organisations such as councils and mortgage lenders sell property at auction because it is regarded as a fair and transparent way to sell property and establish the market value. For these types of organisations, ensuring that the best price is achieved is essential to their obligations. For example, a mortgage lender has an obligation to the former owner to achieve the highest price for their property, and the lender will want to achieve the best price for its own sake, as it will want to avoid a shortfall on any outstanding debt. Councils also have a statutory duty (Section 123 of the Local Government Act, 1972) to achieve the best consideration reasonably obtainable when disposing of its property.

Chapter Summary

This chapter has looked at the main reasons why people buy property at auction. Buying property at auction offers people a wide selection of properties not normally sold through estate agents. Properties at auction are usually sold for a discounted price and allow the buyer to complete a sale quickly. Buying a property at auction offers certainty of sale and is a transparent process that determines the market value of a property.

Expert Tip

Buying at auction is a great way to buy property – it can be cheaper and you have a wider choice. However, the process is much quicker than most people are used to and the contract is also legally binding. It is critical to have everything in place prior to bidding to ensure the sale completes on schedule. People can (and do) get caught out buying at auction – make sure you're not one of them!

Watch Point

Many people buy property at auction because they believe it will be cheaper. This is not always the case. Auction properties can, at times, sell for more than the market value due to the excitement and buzz of the auction room.

CHAPTER 3
The Business of Property Auctions

'A lot of people still think auctions are underground secret dens and are wrongly suspicious of the process . . . buying at auction offers a quick, transparent and immediate sale . . . increasingly people are starting to understand more about buying at auction and why it's so good for the vendor and the buyer'

(Andrew Binstock, Auction House London)

Property auction houses often seem to have a mystical air about them. Hidden from public view and usually not located on the high street, auction houses appear to be 'secret dens' which sell 'secret properties'. However, property auction houses are, in fact, property sales agents. The only difference between a property auction house and an estate agent is that they sell properties at auction! Similarly to an estate agent, an auction house works on behalf of the vendor to sell the property at the best price. This can sometimes be easily forgotten when at auction and the auctioneer is being very friendly with you – but it is important to always remember that the auctioneer works on behalf of the person selling the property.

Property auction houses are in the business of selling properties. The main difference you will find with an auction house and an estate agent is the type of property they sell. Auction houses tend to specialise in repossessions, unmodernised properties, probate sales, building sites, receiver sales and unusual properties. Perhaps this is why auction houses are often seen as a 'special breed' of property agent – and they seem to exude some sort of magical aura around them.

The property had been for sale on the market previously with a price of £500,000 but had failed to sell. It was then passed to us to sell . . .

Admittedly when we were instructed, the property benefited from planning permission for the house to be knocked down and replaced by a new build scheme, but the guide price was £750,000. Given the property had failed to sell previously at £500,000 we were a bit worried if it would make that much money or even sell. The property attracted a lot of media attention and we got some different characters to the auction – we even had some minor celebrities in the room. The property sold for £1.12 million in the end which was 50 per cent more than the guide. (Andrew Binstock, Auction House London)

Behind the scenes at an auction house

To most property auction buyers auction houses seem to magically appear every six to eight weeks with a catalogue stuffed full of properties to sell on a big sale day and then they seem to disappear again. However, the reality is that the business of property auctions is much more involved – it requires a huge amount of effort, preparation and organisation to actually get to the end point of a successful auction sale day.

Turning unknown properties into saleable products

'Auctions are a constant cycle that start and end every seven weeks. You are always getting ready for auction day and then immediately the cycle starts and ends again. You look to sell around fifty properties in a seven week cycle and they are completely unknown properties which you then have to know inside out to be able to sell.'

(Andrew Binstock, Auction House London)

Every auction house works according to a set schedule, which starts and ends with the auction sale day. In the run up to sale day an incredible amount of effort and work goes into transforming an unknown property into a known quantity which the auctioneer can then sell to the public. To be able to sell a property at auction requires a great deal of work in a short space of time: property details need to be gathered, verified and written, solicitors need to be chased to provide legal information, guide prices and reserve prices need to be set, questions need to be asked and answered and all paperwork needs to be prepared. This all needs to happen alongside the marketing of the property, production of the catalogue, preparation of viewing schedules, answering buyer questions, dealing with any pre-auction offers and negotiations with vendors. Behind the scenes the auction house works incredibly hard and to challenging deadlines.

Auction house stock

'Being an auctioneer and standing on the rostrum is a role which only happens seven days of the year. The rest of the year my job is spent gaining instructions, organising property details, getting legal packs, scheduling viewings – it's a constant cycle of taking properties on, selling them and taking more on!'

(Andrew Binstock, Auction House London)

Like any retail business, auction houses require stock to sell. This may sound fairly straightforward, but obtaining listings for properties to be sold at auction is a very competitive business indeed. Similarly to estate agents, auction houses must compete for customers – and in the world of property auctions a lot of stock will usually be controlled by asset managers who work on behalf of corporate lenders, officials who act on behalf of public bodies or senior management in large companies. Private individuals do sell properties at auction; however, the bulk of listings at auction mainly come from a few sources rather than many individuals.

Property auction sellers

The reasons why people sell property at auction can vary – but in the main the key people who sell property at auction are housing associations, local authorities, institutional investors, lenders, property investment companies, companies and private persons.

- **Housing associations/Local authorities** commonly use auction to dispose of properties which are deemed financially unviable or surplus to requirements. This can range from ex-council properties such as residential houses to larger sites such as job centres and libraries. These bodies have a public duty to show accountability for their actions and that the best price was achieved for the property. Selling via auction is seen to reflect a fair market price of that property at that moment in time.

- **Banks/Mortgage lenders** regularly use auctions to sell repossessed properties to achieve a quick sale at the highest price. Where possible, many lenders will place a property for sale with an estate agent before; however, in some instances (for example if the property has defects or has not sold despite being marketed for a considerable period of time), the property will end up for sale at auction. This enables the lender to quickly recoup monies owed (repossessions at auction usually have a sales completion date of fourteen days) and can also show they have acted to achieve the highest price possible.

- **Institutional investors** use property auctions to dispose of investments in an accountable and efficient manner to achieve the best price. Assets may have been held for income generation or capital gains and the disposal at auction ensures the market value of the asset is achieved.

- **Property investment companies** use auctions to dispose of property that no longer fits with their investment aims, or that has now matured to the level where a sale is required. Many investment companies will specialise in a particular sector of the market (for example, properties with regulated tenants) and thus, when the property becomes available, it is most likely that it will require considerable work: this makes it an ideal candidate for auction.

- **Companies** often use auctions to dispose of the business premises they occupy under a 'sale-and-leaseback' agreement, to raise capital or relieve themselves of surplus sites. Tenanted sites are attractive to those looking for income yields, although the value of the occupied property is reliant on the status of the tenant and their financial standing.

- **Private persons** tend to use property auctions when a quick sale is required, if a property has a known defect or is difficult to value. Most private clients who sell at auction do so due to forced circumstances (for example, if there is a need to raise funds quickly, or the property would not sell easily on the open market). Selling a property at auction allows the vendor a quick, secure sale.

How clients choose the auction house they sell with will depend on a number of factors including service levels, price agreements and market share. Statistical sales success is an incredibly important indicator for auction houses to attract clients, for it displays their success in the business of selling properties.

Statistical success

Sales performance and revenue raised is critical to the success of an auction house. The saying 'the proof of the pudding is in the eating' is nowhere more true than when analysing an auction house's sales statistics to ascertain the success of their business. Unlike estate agent's sales, property auction houses' results are public and visible for all to see and scrutinise – and that includes their competitors. At the end of an auction sale it is usual for the auction house to release the final figures, which will disclose the total amount raised, the total number of lots offered and the total number of lots sold. These figures will then be used to produce the success rate, which is presented as a percentage.

An auction held in London has the following sales figures:

		Lots Offered	26
Auctioneer	Athawes Son & Co.	Lots Sold Prior	8
Auction Date	29/01/2013	Lots Sold in Room	9
Venue	Grand Connaught Rooms, Great Queen Street, London, WC2B 5DA	Total Lots Sold	17
		Percent Sold	66%
Start Time	13:00	Total Raised	£2,061,100

(Source: eigroup.co.uk)

From the sales figures for Athawes Son & Co. it can be seen that from a total of twenty-six lots offered, eight were sold prior to auction and nine were sold in the room. The total of the seventeen lots sold from the original twenty-six lots offered means 66 per cent of the stock was sold, raising a total of £2,061,100.

This may be compared with a larger auction house which held an auction in London the previous month:

		Lots Offered	187
Auctioneer	Barnard Marcus	Lots Sold Prior	23
Auction Date	18/12/2012	Lots Sold in Room	98
Venue	Grand Connaught Rooms, Great Queen Street, London, WC2B 5DA	Total Lots Sold	142
		Percent Sold	76%
Start Time	11:00	Total Raised	£20,914,050

(Source: eigroup.co.uk)

The sales figures for Barnard Marcus show that, from a total of 187 lots offered, twenty-three lots sold prior to auction and ninety-eight sold in the room. This gives a total of 121 lots sold before and in the room. However, it is very common for properties to be sold post-auction and in this case a further twenty-one lots were sold after auction to give a total of 142 sold. This means 76 per cent of the stock was sold raising a total of £20,914,050.

What is key to note from the above statistics is that because of the difference in size of the auction houses and the number of lots offered, a direct comparison of sales revenue or number of lots sold is not meaningful.

However, a direct comparison can be made with the percentage figure (per cent sold) which is the success rate of an auction house.

Industry averages show the success rate of an auction house to be 75 per cent, hence this is the goal which many auction houses will seek to beat. The sales statistics below are from the leading auctioneer in the UK – and with such impressive sales statistics it is not hard to see why.

		Lots Offered	267
Auctioneer	Allsop Residential	Lots Sold Prior	13
Auction Date	18/12/2012	Lots Sold in Room	186
Venue	Park Lane Hotel, Piccadilly, London, W1J 7BX	Total Lots Sold	233
		Percent Sold	88%
Start Time	09:45	Total Raised	£41,973,750

(Source: eigroup.co.uk)

The sales figures for Allsop Residential show that, from a total of 267 lots offered, thirteen lots were sold prior to auction and 186 were sold in the room. Again, a number of lots were sold post-auction (thirty-four) taking the total sold to 233 lots. This means that 88 per cent of the stock was sold, raising a total of £41,973,750.

Looking at the sales statistics you would be forgiven for thinking that most vendors would just choose the biggest and most successful auction house to sell their lots. However, auction houses vary in terms of the stock they are known for, the geographical focus and also the relationship they have with certain clientele. This is similar to shopping at the supermarket – not everyone chooses Tesco just because it's the biggest or the most successful.

Let us look at the different types of auction houses.

Types of auction houses

Auction houses are rather like the stock they sell – they come in varying shapes and sizes. While auction houses are all in the same business there is a different style and culture to every one. You will tend to find most regular auction buyers have favourite auction houses they like to buy from. This could be based on the stock the auction house offers, the service received, the geographical location or the prices at which lots are bought. Auction houses tend to specialise in either residential or commercial sectors, although there is some crossover and a residential auction house will still sell a commercial property and vice versa. The auction house descriptions below are more typical of residential auctioneers who also sell commercial lots.

Large auction houses

Large auction houses typically hold auctions every six to eight weeks and offer approximately 100 to 300 lots per sale. Most of the auctions will be held in Central London locations, but the properties on offer will range nationwide with anything from a hotel in Newcastle to an island off Scotland to a swanky studio flat in Chelsea. Many of these large auction houses take their stock from banks, housing associations, institutional organisations and many other large companies.

These auction houses tend to advertise their property auctions in the mainstream press such as *The Times* and the *Telegraph*. The size and variety of lots on offer, plus the marketing efforts, attract hundreds, if not thousands, of buyers to the sale room. On some occasions, the room can become so packed that potential buyers are literally spilling out of the doors.

Medium auction houses

Medium-sized auction houses usually have regular auctions every six to eight weeks and offer approximately 25 to 100 lots per sale. Many of the auctions will be held in large venues in regional centres, with the properties on offer tending to be located in and around the area. Medium-sized auction houses take instructions from lenders, housing associations, companies and some private individuals.

These auction houses tend to advertise in the local press and attract mainly local residents and regular auction buyers. The number of lots on offer and geographic focus tends to attract buyers who live in or invest in the area.

Small auction houses

Small auction houses are more periodic in their auction dates and offer from 1 to 25 lots per sale. The auctions are likely to be held in pub or hotel function rooms, although it is not unusual for the auction to be held at the property which is being auctioned. Most of the lots will be located in a specific geographic area or will be of a particular type (for example, arable land). Stock will usually come from private individuals and local businesses.

Small auction houses may advertise in the local press; however, word of mouth and mailing list registration are usually sufficient to ensure an interested turnout. Buyers are more likely to be locals to the area.

Types of auction buyers

Property auctions attract a huge variety of people from all walks of life. In previous years the saleroom would mainly have been full of men in the trade. This is changing as auctions have become more popular and increasing numbers of people are attracted to the process of buying property at auction. The main groups who buy at auction are:

- **Property Traders** are always on the lookout for deals they can trade and make a margin on (think Del Boy from *Only Fools and Horses*). Typically male, cash buyers, they work on high volume, profit and speed. Most buy in a 'patch' (area), will have intimate local knowledge and will often bid blind based on price.

- **Property Investors** fall into two camps: capital growth investors and income investors. Capital growth investors are very selective over the type of properties they buy and the areas in which they buy 'Local knowledge' is king to this type of investor as they plan to be owning and holding this asset for the long term. Rental yields may be low, but this is offset by the anticipated future capital appreciation of the property. Income investors buy properties based on rental yield and focus on cash flow. This type of investor will usually have a large portfolio and properties will tend to have a low capital value with high yields to maximise rental returns.

- **Property Developers** focus on the development angle or 'upside' of a property. This group look to develop property for profit. Auctions attract a wide range of developers from multi-millionaire Ferrari drivers to one-man-band builders short on work.

- **Owner-Occupiers** buy to live in the property as a home and buy at auction for the variety, speed and price on offer. Finance is usually required and bids are typically higher due to their emotional attachment to the property.

Auctioneer Anecdote

Auctions attract a diverse audience from private investors to first-time buyers and big developers. We had been instructed to sell a property which attracted my most memorable audience yet. The lot we were to sell was a big, detached property in Oxfordshire. It had quite a lot of land with it and in the grounds was a small industrial park where the former couple who owned the property ran a business. Unfortunately, the couple had since split and the divorce was very acrimonious. The property became the centre of the court battle with both the husband and wife wanting to keep it – but without the other in it!

As no agreement could be reached on who should be awarded the property, the judge insisted the property was sold at public auction. Both the husband and wife wanted to buy the property and were expected to attend and bid. On sale day, I arrived at the auction to conduct proceedings and found the car park to be full. I was very surprised when I found a large section of the car park had been roped off and there was a black helicopter parked in the car park! It turned out the husband had flown in, in his private helicopter.

In the auction room I soon clocked the husband and wife – who were standing at opposite ends of the room. The husband looked like something out of a mafia film as he stood at the back drinking a pint of beer flanked by men dressed in black! The auction was hotly contested with both the husband and wife bidding furiously to gain the winning bid. In the end, the husband won the property at £1.5 million, much to the annoyance of his wife who dramatically flounced out of the room. (Guy Charrison, Network Auctions)

Insider Insight

The stock of an auction house tends to influence the sort of buyers attracted to the sale. Some of the best auction buys can be when a property is mismatched to the auction house and audience (for example, a regional auctioneer selling a property 'out of area').

Chapter Summary

This chapter has looked at the business of property auctions and what happens behind the scenes in the lead up to sale day. Auction houses are often seen as 'secret dens', yet they play a key role in selling property for a wide range of clients. Auction houses are known for selling different properties, which is likely to contribute to their magical aura. Turning unknown properties into known saleable lots requires a great deal of preparation and organisation to ensure a successful sale day. Gaining stock to sell at auction is a competitive business and success rates are key to showing sales performance. Auction houses come in varying shapes and sizes and the main types of auction house have been described along with the main groups of buyers who attend.

Expert Tip

Every auction house has their own cultural style of running the business. Service levels and ways of doing business can vary between auction houses. You should always check with individual auction houses rather than presuming all of them are the same.

Watch Point

The volume of properties auction houses deal with and the deadlines they are working to means very often critical information may not be received until very close to the auction sale day.

CHAPTER 4

Finding and Viewing Auction Property

'I'd love to buy property at auction – but where do you find them? I've seen programmes on TV and read in the paper about it, but it all seems to happen in some sort of secret world which I don't know anything about.'

. (Emma, housewife)

Finding an auction property

To the uninitiated, the world of property auctions seems like some sort of secret underworld – a rather illicit affair where shifty-looking men meet in basements with suitcases stuffed full of money. However, the reality is very different. Property auctions are often held in big, central hotels where once you start attending you can't believe you didn't know it was happening in the first place. Of course, I can't comment on the shifty-looking men – but I can say that cash is no longer accepted as payment for properties due to strict money laundering rules – so put your suitcases away!

The UK property auction market is huge – and definitely not a secret world. In the twelve-month period from January to December 2012 there were a total of 34,065 lots offered at auction. That is equivalent to ninety-three lots being offered for sale at auction every day of the year. Not to mention the sales raised, which were a whopping £3.49 billion according to Essential Information Group.

Auction property is literally all around you – but you have to know how and where to find it. There are three main ways to find auction property: publications, professional subscription and auction house mailing list registration.

Publications

The main publication is *Property Auction News*, which is dedicated to property auctions throughout the UK. This is a paid-for subscription. More details of this can be found at www.propertyauctionnews.co.uk

The *Estates Gazette* is a weekly property publication and features some auction property sales and commentary. Further details can be found at www.estatesgazette.com

Professional Subscription

Essential Information Group (EIG) offers a comprehensive listing of all auction houses and properties being sold at auction in the UK. This is an online resource that charges an annual membership fee. Access to EIG provides up-to-the-minute details on all property auctions happening across the UK, and on some, even allows online access to watch the auctions live. EIG also provides access to many valuable research resources for buying property at auction such as legal documents, land registry comparables and historic data for auction sales. Further details can be found at www.eigroup.co.uk

Auction House Mailing List

Most auction houses have a mailing list which you can register for, be updated about upcoming auction dates and receive auction catalogues. Auction houses are located all over the UK. Many of the larger auction houses are based in London, but they deal with properties across the country. There is a comprehensive list of UK property auction houses provided in the Appendix (Auctioneer Directory) on p. 224.

Registration with auction houses is open to all, and, in the majority of cases, auction catalogues are free (remember: this is the equivalent of asking for a company's sales brochure). Auction catalogues can also be found online at many of the auction houses' own websites and you can arrange to be alerted via email when a new catalogue or sale date is scheduled.

Alternative places to find repossessed property

People often attend auctions looking to buy repossessed property. Repossessions are a sad fact of the housing market in the UK, and one which looks set to increase when interest rates start to rise. Repossessed properties are usually sold quickly to repay debts owed by the former owner to the lending bank. This can mean the repossessed property may be sold more cheaply, owing to the timescales involved. However, while the property may be sold at a relatively low price, it is important to note that the lender is obliged to get the best possible price – that is, a reasonable and achievable amount for the property. Lenders need to recoup their losses wherever possible and generally they will do this by accepting the highest offer.

Repossessed properties, while being priced competitively, may also require works to improve the standard of the property (or in some cases, to even make them habitable). This may range from minor modernisation to full-scale refurbishment of the property depending on the condition. A further point to note with repossessed properties is, in my experience, the seemingly uncanny nature of many of these properties to have had illegal or shoddy work done to them. At first sight, many of these properties appear to require just light, cosmetic works, however, I have found countless repossessed properties have 'hidden' issues ranging from faulty wiring to problematic plumbing and illegal building works. This can be very expensive to put right and is not always apparent at the outset.

Repossessed properties can be found for sale in a number of high street estate agents and also online at websites such as www.whitehotproperty.co.uk (where they are known as 'Public Notice Property'). Another way to find repossessions is via the public notices section in local newspapers. By law, estate agents must notify the general public of any offer which has been received and accepted on a repossessed property. Once the notice has been publicised, there is then a deadline date by which any increased offer must be received. The notice will display the property details, the offer that has been accepted and the deadline date by which any improved final offers must be received.

It is important to note that, when looking to buy a repossessed property, you must be in a 'proceedable' position. That means you must have the finances organised and any deposit funds in place to buy the repossessed property. It is quite usual for the estate agent to ask for proof of deposit funds and funding before an offer is submitted for consideration to the lender. This is because if the bank does accept the offer for the property the timescale for sale exchange and completion will be quicker than usual (six to eight weeks being the norm).

The tell-tale signs of a repossessed property

Repossessed properties are often marketed by estate agents in advance of their being entered for sale at auction. If the repossession does not sell in a certain time period, or if there are some issues with the property which make it unsuitable for an estate agent sale, then it will be entered for sale at auction.

Repossessions listed with an estate agent do not have flashing neon lights, but there are many tell-tale signs which give the game away in the estate agent particulars of a repossessed property. The key signs are:

- In the property particulars: 'chain free/being sold on behalf of a corporate client'.

- In the exterior property photographs: an A4 sheet of paper usually located at the front of the property affixed to the window/door. This will display details that the property has been repossessed.

- In the internal property photographs: in the bathroom and kitchen there will usually be stickers or coloured striped tape around the water and gas appliances. This shows the system has been drained down.

Repossessions may make up a sizeable chunk of the properties sold at auction – but there is also so much more on offer. The key way to unlock the excitement of buying property at auction is to obtain the property auction catalogue.

The property auction catalogue

Property auction catalogues are usually released by auction houses two to three weeks before the date of the auction sale – which doesn't give you long to get everything in order. The catalogue will usually be available in both printed and electronic form. While there may be slight deviations between the auction houses, property auction catalogues will generally have a similar amount of detail on the property to be auctioned. It is important to remember the property auction catalogue is the equivalent of the auction house's sales brochure – the catalogue contains the properties they want to sell and which they are hoping you want to buy.

The auction catalogue contains all of the properties which the auctioneer will be selling on that particular auction date. The entries, known as lots, are listed in numerical order and the details of each lot will usually contain a guide price, the property address, a brief description of the property, viewing arrangements and a photograph.

A typical catalogue entry for a property may look like this.
(Source: Network Auctions, 2013)

How to read the auction catalogue entry

Auction catalogue entries provide the key basic information about a property being sold. Unlike estate agent particulars, there are no room dimensions or gallery of photos to peruse. This can make the decision about whether you want to buy a property quite difficult as there is not a lot of information provided. However, there are tips and tricks where you can find out more, which I will outline later. For now, we will concentrate on the auction catalogue entry, which will comprise:

- **Address.** The auction catalogue entry will provide the address of the property being sold.

- **Photograph.** There is generally one photograph provided of the external appearance of the property.

- **Details.** The catalogue will provide a brief description of the property being sold. This will usually include how many rooms the property has or the size of the site (if land is being sold), the tenure of the property (whether it is leasehold or freehold) and whether the property is vacant or tenanted (and, if tenanted, the length of lease and rents being received). Usually there are details of who is selling the property (for example, if it is a council disposal or on behalf of the mortgagees). On occasion the auctioneer may add some additional notes such as any planning potential or condition of the property (for example, the property requires a full scheme of modernisation).

- **Guide price.** The auctioneer will provide a guide price for the property which indicates to the buyers what they might expect the property to sell for at auction.

Guide prices can be notoriously difficult to judge, but guide prices are just that – they are simply set as a *guide* to the price you may pay for the property at auction.

- **Viewing arrangements.** The auctioneer will detail how the property can be viewed. This may be by direct auctioneer contact, a specialist viewing company, or with a local estate agent who works in partnership with the auction house. They may be listed as 'joint auctioneer' or 'offered in conjunction with . . .'

Tips and tricks about the auction catalogue

As previously mentioned, the auction catalogue is the equivalent of a company sales brochure. It is important to bear this in mind when looking through a catalogue as it has been carefully designed with the sale of the properties in mind. The catalogue has been put together so that buyers will read through it, like what they see and buy a property. The catalogue is *not* a random collection of properties for sale – there is a whole sales process going on behind the scenes.

The property auction catalogue – order is important!

The catalogue will carry a quantity of lots, numbered in the order in which they will be sold on auction day. Thus 'Lot 1' will be sold first and will appear as the first property in the catalogue, the following lots will be sold in subsequent order on the sale day. It is useful to remember that auction houses spend a long time designing the order of a catalogue to ensure interest levels are maintained in the sale room and to ensure people look through the rest of the catalogue. While you can bid on the telephone and by proxy at auction, actually attending the auction sale day is still the most popular way in which people buy. Therefore, it is important for the auction house to maintain attendance levels and the energy of the room as much as possible throughout the sale day.

It is often the case that auction houses put the lots which they believe will be the most popular towards the front of the catalogue. Typically lot 1 will be a 'hook' to ensure plenty of people get excited by the catalogue and also attend the auction early, hoping to pick up a bargain. This ensures lots of people are in the auction room from the start and a positive energy and buzz are created. The anticipated popular lots will be interspersed with the less popular lots to manage the momentum in the room, spread energy levels and also ensure the best price is achieved for the properties in the room on that day.

In general, large auction houses will start by offering London properties first, before moving on to different regions throughout the day. A typical auction sale day of a large size auction house may start with twenty to thirty lots in London, then move on to the Home Counties, before moving to properties for sale in the south-west, the Midlands, the north-west, the north-east, Wales, Scotland and Northern Ireland. Some auction houses may also use 'reverse hooks', in which they hold back some of the most popular properties until the very end to ensure bidders attend auctions towards the end of the day when the room may have quietened down. This has the result of encouraging higher attendance levels in the room and the possibility of sparking off a bidding war which may encourage a higher price to be paid for the property.

It is important to remember that auctioneers are looking to achieve the best price for the seller and thus a packed auction room with interested parties and high levels of audience participation are required to achieve their goal.

Sleeper lots

Auction houses go to great lengths to put together a catalogue that will interest buyers on the day of the sale and also create enough curiosity to get them to flick through the rest of the catalogue (no mean feat if you have a catalogue of over 100 properties!).

This means that auction houses have to spend a long time thinking about their audience – how to get them to stay longer, bid higher and read further. It's important to remember the auction catalogue is a sales brochure, and so like any great sales team they want to encourage their customers to buy from them.

A 'sleeper lot' is one which has been entered into the catalogue in a less prominent position – but which, by virtue of a low guide price or local knowledge, becomes unexpectedly popular with viewers. Sleeper lots can take auction houses by surprise, as the demand for the property surges and this creates an exciting buzz which generates a great burst of energy in the room on the day.

TIP

If you like the look of the first lot in the auction catalogue, the likelihood is so will many others. Be prepared to spend considerably more than the guide price if you want to be in with a chance of success.

AUCTIONEER ANECDOTE

 LOT 25 By Order of Executors
88 Lilford Road, Camberwell, London, SE5 9HR

A Vacant Leasehold Three Bedroom Mid Terrace House

GUIDE PRICE £17,500+

Tenure
Leasehold. There are 8 years remaining on the lease

Location
The property is situated in the south east London residential area of Camberwell close to local shops and restaurants and within close proximity to the open spaces of Myatts Field. Transport links are provided by Loughborough Junction rail station.

Description
The property comprises a three bedroom mid terrace house arranged over ground and first floors. The property requires a full program of refurbishment.

Accommodation
The property has not been internally inspected. We understand that the internal arrangement is as follows:

Ground Floor
Two Reception Rooms
Kitchen/Breakfast Room
Bathroom

First Floor
Three Bedrooms
Bathroom

Exterior
The property benefits from a rear garden

Note
The property is occupied by squatters and therefore there will be no viewings

Lilford Road, Camberwell (Source: Auction House London, 2011)

We were instructed to sell a house in Lilford Road, Camberwell, London. The property was in a dire condition; it was squatted and even missing a wall! It was also leasehold with only eight years left on the lease. The guide and reserve was set at £17,500. The vendor was hoping we could achieve £20,000, and we were hoping we could actually sell it for more like £40,000–50,000. The property ended up attracting a lot of media attention and on auction day we were all blown away by the frantic bidding. Most lots are sold within two minutes, but with this lot the bidding went on for over twenty minutes. The property eventually got knocked down at £100,500 which was far more than what we or the vendor ever thought it would make. (Andrew Binstock, Auction House London)

Guide prices set tantalisingly low

Guide prices for properties sold at auction can seem mind-blowingly cheap. In fact there are several auction houses who deliberately set their guide prices incredibly low to tempt buyers in. What happens is that because the guide price is set *so* low, this attracts the attention of a huge number of interested people who think they may be able to buy the property for a very cheap price. This then increases the competition to buy the property and the final sale price will usually end up nowhere near the guide price first set. This practice is not illegal, as the whole point of selling a property at auction is for the people in the room on the day to dictate the market value of that property. The key point to bear in mind is that the guide price is there to *guide* people; it is not the price you should *expect* to pay – it is purely an indication.

Guide prices are not set in stone and occasionally the guide price of a property can be altered prior to being sold at auction. The guide price will sometimes be changed according to the level of interest which has been shown in a lot prior to auction. If the property has proved particularly popular at viewings then the auctioneer may increase the guide price, or, if the lot has not had much interest prior to auction, the guide price may be reduced to try to stimulate interest in the lot ahead of the sale day.

Before you get disheartened by thinking guide prices are unreliable, it is important to note that guide prices are set according to strict requirements. Auction houses cannot make up the guide prices and then change their minds willy-nilly, nor can they set a guide price and then not sell the property within the guide price region. Guide prices are dictated by the 'reserve price' on the lot. Every lot being sold at auction has a reserve price – that is, the lowest price at which the vendor is willing to sell. This reserve price is often not disclosed to potential buyers before auction, but it does have a major impact on the guide price of a property. Guide prices are almost always set within 5–10 per cent of the reserve price. When you remember this rule, it is very easy to work out what the reserve price of a property is. If a property does not reach the reserve price set by the vendor, then the property will not be sold. This is regardless of whether the guide price was reached in the room – if the reserve is not met, the property will not be sold. This is similar to when you see people selling items on eBay – the reserve price is the price below which the vendor will not sell the item.

Is the photo really a photo of that property?

It sounds daft, but it has been known on quite a few occasions for the photograph of the property being sold not actually to be of the property being sold. Auctioneers take great care to ensure they provide correct details and photographs in the catalogue, but mix-ups and mistakes do happen. It is also important to check that the photograph used is a recent shot that portrays the current condition of the property. It is not unheard of for a property photograph to be provided of what the property looked like some years ago, before it was burned down! Again, these are extreme examples – but it happens. This is why it is imperative that you view the property and do not rely on the particulars provided in the auction catalogue as they may not always be entirely accurate.

Where is the property really located?

The address of a property should be fairly straightforward,

and in most cases it is. However, it has been known (especially in London boroughs) for a property to be described as located in a more desirable location than where it actually is. This is because a cheap property in a more desirable location will tempt more people into viewing the property and hook in more potential buyers. While this sounds a far-fetched example, it is important to note that particular streets and postcodes can be subject to interpretation, and some 'creative geographic licence' may have been applied when listing the property address.

What state is it in?

Most lot descriptions will not detail the condition of the property, although there may be some clues in the particulars. Key watchwords to look out for are: 'would benefit from updating', 'short lease', 'planning enforcement', 'title issues', 'structural movement' and 'further investigation is required'. These all indicate known issues with the property and start to give you some idea of the problems (as well as the budget you will need to set aside to resolve them).

Are auction properties too good to be true?

Auctions are a great source of bargain-priced properties – but the old adage rings very true when it comes to property at auction: if it seems too good to be true . . . it probably is!

Properties sold at auction usually come with a huge amount of baggage and history which you wouldn't ordinarily find with properties being sold by an estate agent. Most property at auction has a history and a story to tell and most of the time it will be a tale of woe which needs to be put right by the new owner. Invariably, having a happy ending to the story costs money and takes time – and these all need to be factored in when deciding whether to buy a property at auction. The key is to weigh up the pros and cons – and work out how a 'too good to be true' property can be made to exist in reality.

LEGAL INSIGHT

From a legal point of view, one of the main drawbacks of buying at auction is that the vendors of the property do not (usually) answer any written enquiries whatsoever about the property being sold. In a normal sale, the buyer (and buyer's solicitor) has the opportunity to raise questions about the property being sold with the seller and their solicitor. The answers given by the seller to those important questions form part of the 'contractual representations' made by the seller when the buyer enters into a contract to purchase the property. The trouble with auction sales is that, generally speaking, there is very little information provided within the auction pack from those people who previously owned the property. The standard auction conditions of sale usually prevent the buyer (or buyer's solicitor) from raising any questions whatsoever about the property once the hammer has fallen. (Michael John Hayward, solicitor)

What to do when you find a property you like in the auction catalogue

Once you've got the catalogue and have found a property you are interested in, you need to get your skates on, because you won't have long before the property is being sold at auction. Over the next couple of weeks you will have to pull out all the stops to ensure you are ready and able to bid on the property at auction.

The first step is to view the auction property which we will discuss next.

Viewing the auction property

Viewing a property that is going to auction is rather different from when you view a property with an estate agent.

1. The viewing times are normally set by the auction house and you will have to fit in with their schedule.

2. There will usually only be three to six viewings before auction.

3. The viewing will usually be a block viewing for all interested people to attend.

Viewing arrangements

In the auction catalogue there will normally be a page which is devoted to the viewing arrangements of the property. This will typically be arranged by lot number and will state the day, date and time when the property will be available to view. Be aware that unlike estate agents who are selling a property, most people who conduct viewings are employed purely as 'key holders', and will not know any further details about the property. This can cause confusion for buyers as they are used to the person showing them around knowing something about the property. In the case of auction properties, this is often not the case. In the main, the person who is showing the property is purely there to open the door and to collect a list of the names and contact details of the people who have attended the viewing.

It is also worth bearing in mind that the person who is showing the property may not even be employed by the auction house directly. Some large auction houses use the services of viewing companies, which liaise directly with the auction house and will organise the viewings on their behalf. This means that any questions which you have about the property need to be directed to the auction house rather than the viewing company or the person conducting the viewing.

Property viewings are usually held two or three times per week, in 20–30-minute slots. It is best practice to call the auction house prior to a viewing to confirm the viewing details. It can happen that a property gets withdrawn from sale, or the keys have not arrived, or all manner of other things that may prevent a viewing from happening. Given the tight deadlines involved it is always best to check before you set off to ensure you do not have a wasted journey.

It is important to arrive in good time for the viewing slot as the person conducting it will have a strict schedule to keep to and often will be unable to extend appointments. It is best to get to a viewing early so that you can take full advantage of the time available to look around the property. Half an hour is not a long time to check the property before you potentially part with tens or hundreds of thousands of pounds!

Property viewings are usually held on a block basis – it is an open house for that time period and anybody who is interested in the property will need to arrive at the scheduled time to view it. If you arrive in good time to view you will normally be able to tell the property being sold because there will be a small crowd of people gathering outside the front door.

TIP

It is best to arrive early at a property viewing to survey the outside of the property. Any external issues or questions should be checked thoroughly on the internal viewing.

Auction houses use block viewings for two reasons:

1. It's an effective use of time (it's easier to tell people when the viewing appointment is, rather than trying to please everybody with their desired time).

2. It's a psychological tool – block viewings start to instil the competitive nature into people from the outset by gathering them together with other interested parties at the property. This gets people into the frame of mind needed in the auction room when people are bidding against each other to buy the property.

In the beginning, viewing property with lots of other people around can feel quite off-putting and in some cases quite overwhelming – especially if it's a small property that is popular and there are hordes of people all trying to view at the same time. It can prove rather difficult to think privately when surrounded by so many other people who are all potentially interested in buying the same property as you. However, it is critical to ensure you see all you need to see, and find out all you need to know when viewing a property going to auction as you do not have long to make a final decision before attempting a purchase. It is also worth bearing in mind that just because a property may look popular at a viewing (with literally queues of people cramming in) it does not necessarily mean that all of those people will want to buy the property and actually attend the auction to bid. So don't be put off by a property just because it looks 'too popular' – things are not always as they seem!

TIP
A popular property viewing does not always mean high prices at auction.

Do your homework *before* you view
The best route to property auction success is thorough research – and this means even *before* you view the property. As we have seen previously, the property auction catalogue provides minimal detail. The best way to use these property details is as a starting point for your own research. The catalogue entry displays what property is available and at what guide price – what you need to do next is the necessary research to decide if you even want to view the property.

Pre-viewing research
Before you get in the car, or even *think* about getting in the car to start your auction property adventure, you need to be clear about the property offered for sale.

This means undertaking research on two key factors:

1. Location of property.

2. The actual property being sold.

Location of property – Google it!
The advent of Google Maps has made checking out property so much easier and can be done from the comfort of

your armchair. Google Maps is a fantastic tool for thoroughly researching the location of the property and is the most time- and cost-effective way of conducting the initial property research. The key things you should be analysing when using Google Maps is the proximity of the property to transport links, major employment areas, schools, shops, bars, restaurants and any other such amenities which you and people in the local area would be attracted by (and also put off by). Ordinarily, a property which is close to a train station would command a premium; however, if the property is *too* close to the train station or the tracks run along the back garden perimeter then this will reduce the value of the property. The same is true for major road networks and other commercial entities – being close adds to the value of the property, but being *too* close will reduce the value of the property.

The satellite images from Google Maps can prove very useful in showing the outlying area of a property and allow you to see things you wouldn't ordinarily see from the ground. The satellite view may indicate potential areas of interest which require further investigation when attending the viewing. For example, the satellite image may show an unidentified large building close to the property you are thinking of buying. This should be noted down and researched further when attending the viewing to be sure it is not a building which may have a detrimental effect on the area or the value of the property.

Google Maps' Streetview function enables you to 'walk along the street' as though you are actually in the street. This is a fantastic tool which can save a lot of time and allows you to learn so much about the area without even leaving the house! While Streetview shots are not of the street today, they give a great indication as to what the property and the surrounding area is like. By using Streetview you can view the property externally and get a feel of the street, which will give you a good idea about what the area is like. It is worth noting down any 'for sale' or 'to let' boards and any properties which appear to be undergoing works or show signs of disrepair. When you attend the property for a viewing, these items should be checked to compare the current situation to give you a clearer idea of the area.

CASE STUDY: THE CLIFF TOP PROPERTY THAT WAS NEVER VIEWED

Sue Diamond's auction purchase hit the headlines when she successfully bid by phone for Ridgemont House, a cliff-top six-bedroom detached property in Torquay, Devon. It was a property she had never seen. Despite the auction particulars warning prospective buyers that the property was severely structurally damaged and might be beyond economic repair, Diamond paid £154,500 for the property *without* viewing it or commissioning a survey.

Just days after the auction, the property was hit by a landslide, leaving it 50 yards from the edge of a vertical 300-foot drop into the sea. Diamond claimed the property was uninhabitable and worth only £3,500 and refused to complete on the sale. The owner of Ridgemont House was forced to live in a caravan and took legal action against Diamond for the non-completion. A judge ordered Diamond to pay the owner what she owed and placed a legal charge on Diamond's London home, plus 8 per cent interest annually. A year later Diamond was evicted from her home in London so that it could be sold and the owner of Ridgemont House paid. (*Daily Mail*, 8 February 2013)

Actual property being sold – check the legal paperwork before viewing

This sounds an odd thing to do, but it is critical to know as much as you can about the actual property being sold *before* you view. Most auction houses allow buyers to download legal documents from their site, or can email interested buyers when paperwork becomes available. Checking the paperwork prior to viewing will provide you with vital information about the property to ensure it is the sort of property you are thinking of buying. This does not have to be to the level that a solicitor would check, but is more of a fact-finding mission about the property and should be treated as an introductory overview of the property. You do not require a law degree to check the following:

- **Energy Performance Certificate (EPC).** These are brilliant fact sheets about the property that quickly tell you, at a glance, the size of the property, whether the property has double-glazing, insulation, electric heating and/or gas central heating. The EPC will also give you an indication of further measures which could be undertaken to improve the energy efficiency rating. This is critical information as it gives insight into what works may be necessary to bring the property up to scratch and can help you to start formulating an outline refurbishment budget.

- **Property title.** The title information comes from Land Registry data and will provide you with the tenure information for the property. If the property is leasehold, this will be shown on the title documents and will detail the length of the lease and the amount of ground rent paid per annum. This is critical information as the length of the lease on a property will ultimately dictate the value. Leases less than eighty years in length will need to be extended in the future for the value to be increased/protected and this will come at considerable cost (depending on the lease length and freeholder). Towards the end of the title entry, previous sale information will also usually be provided along with any financial charges registered against the property, such as a mortgage lender.

- **Property title plan.** The title plan of the property is derived from Land Registry data and will show the boundaries of the property and any land included in the title. This is a simple line drawing which outlines what is included in the property being sold.

LEGAL INSIGHT

In addition to checking the terms of the Registered Lease you should check the service charge information. Copies of service charge accounts and previous invoices paid on the property should be included within the auction pack for the last three years. Without proper service charge information the buyer cannot form a balanced view as to whether the property in question is being effectively managed and maintained and cannot ascertain what the property is likely to cost in the future. (Michael John Hayward, solicitor)

Expert Tip

Buyers should check how long the seller has been the registered owner of the property on the Land Registry title. Mortgage lenders adopt a Lending Code which says they won't actually offer a mortgage to a buyer if the seller has owned the property for less than six months. Always be aware of sellers who are looking for a 'quick turnaround' on a property they've only just bought because you might be refused a mortgage by your lender to purchase it. (Michael John Hayward, solicitor)

CASE STUDY: POWYS, WALES – THE CASE OF THE COTTAGE PART-BUILT ON WHOSE LAND?

A cottage in Wales for auction.

In November 2012, a cute Victorian detached cottage was entered into an auction with a guide price of just £8,000. The cottage was in a stunning location in the foothills of Mount Snowdon in Wales. The property was detailed as needing some upgrading, but benefited from a large area of woodland to the rear, an attached store, an open-fronted log store and a parking area. In the catalogue particulars the auctioneer had noted: 'We understand that part of the accommodation lies within an extension built on land that is not included in the title'.

A study of the legal paperwork soon revealed the issue to be a title problem: a part of the cottage building appeared to be built on land that did not belong to the title plan of the cottage. However, the issue was odd, as the title plan showed a large area of land which the cottage owned and which measured approximately an acre. This land ran alongside the public road which the cottage adjoined. The outline of the registered land was almost a straight square all the way around, apart from a tiny, unexplained 'bump' halfway into where the cottage was located. This meant that part of the cottage had been built on land which was not included in the title plan – and therefore did not belong to the cottage.

The property was a repossession and the previous owners had paid £127,500 for the cottage in 2007. Five years later the property, with its auction guide price of £8,000 in 2012, was now worth just a fraction of the previous sale price – not good news for the bank or the previous owners. The legal documents showed the bank's solicitors had engaged in lengthy correspondence with the Land Registry about the title to the cottage as it was believed an error had been made in an earlier document. It was argued that the tiny bump in the title plan – which was the bit where part of the cottage building was located – was a mistake. However, without a missing document from 1906 the issue could not be resolved satisfactorily. This meant that whoever bought the cottage could potentially be buying a building where part of the accommodation was owned by someone else! Given that the cottage had been built in about 1900, with the extension built in the 1970s, it was highly unlikely that any claim to part of the building would now surface. However, because of this title plan issue, the property could not be deemed as 'suitable security' for most banks to lend money against.

This meant the property was mainly of interest to cash buyers, and those who were willing to take a risk on the title plan being a mistake rather than somebody else owning a part of the building. This substantially reduced the value of the cottage and it sold in November 2012 for a price of just £40,500. Comparable properties in the area regularly fetch in excess of £110,000.

How to conduct a successful auction property viewing

Most people spend more time thinking about a new brand of toothpaste than they do viewing a property they are thinking of buying. When buying property with an estate agent it is possible to have repeated viewings, with time to negotiate items with vendors, and there is always the chance, should you decide, that you no longer want to buy the property. However, when buying a property at auction the process is very different. Viewings will be shorter, scheduled by the auction house and with a crowd of other interested buyers; legal documents will be provided ahead of sale and there is minimal opportunity to ask questions of the vendor (especially if it is a lender who has never lived at the property). Most importantly, when buying at auction, once you have successfully bid on a property there is no get-out clause to fall back on. This means you should make the most of every viewing opportunity and ensure you get as much information about the property as possible. The research you do will enable you to make a clear and informed decision about the property before you commit yourself to buying.

As we have seen, there is a lot of research to be undertaken prior to viewing a property. When you attend the property viewing, this desk research will stand you in good stead to ask the right questions and check on any issues your research may have highlighted for further investigation. This is all part and parcel of your role as a property detective – and it is at the viewing that you need to be extra vigilant and on the lookout for any hidden clues which are not immediately obvious. The role of the property detective will be discussed in more detail later – but for now, let us be a surveyor.

LEGAL TIP

When viewing the property, take along a copy of the Land Registry title plan to make absolutely sure that the full extent of the property which you intend to buy is accurately shown on the Land Registry plan. (Michael John Hayward, solicitor)

Be a 'surveyor' at the property viewing

A property viewing will typically last thirty minutes, which means it is critical to make the most of the time available. Preparation and organisation are paramount. When surveying a property there are several key areas you should examine. Given that there will probably be a number of other people at the viewing, it is important to ensure you don't get sidetracked and all information is written down and photographed to enable you to make a firm decision.

Key items to take on a viewing:

- a strong pair of shoes (most auction properties require work).

- a tape measure.

- a camera.

- a notepad.

- a torch.

- a pair of binoculars (to check roof, gutter, chimney).

- a portable ladder (to access loft space).

- the contact details of auctioneer.

- research notes for further investigation in the area (for example, an unidentified building).

How to conduct a property survey – a checklist

It is advisable to employ the services of a qualified surveyor to check the property. However, for the first property viewing you should act like one yourself. While you may not be a professional the checklist on the next few pages, although not exhaustive, will provide you with a good overview of areas that should be checked. It is essential to take notes on the condition of the property and these should always be supported by photos to allow you to refer back. Ideally, photos should be taken of the whole property externally and also internally on a room-by-room basis. Specific areas of interest should be photographed in detail along with any items of repair or areas that require further investigation.

- **Roof**
  - Check the timbers and look for signs of bowing.

  - Examine if there are any slipped or missing tiles.

  - Inspect the condition of the felt or asphalt, and if it is a flat roof check for signs of standing water.

  - If it is a house or top-floor flat, assess the existing eaves height to see if a mansard or loft conversion may be possible.

  - Check all ceilings for evidence of leaks from the roof and any unexplained patches of discoloration.

- **Plumbing**
  - Check the location and working nature of stopcocks.

  - Investigate the age, location and condition of the boiler.

  - Calculate the lie of the pipes if you are considering relocating things.

  - Check external pipework and condition, i.e. guttering and soil stack.

  - If the property is a flat in a large block, check if the heating and hot water is individual per flat or part of a communal system.

- **Electrics**
  - Check the age and state of the fuses and main board.

  - Check the position and quantity of wall sockets.

- Note that wiring may become illegal under current regulations if any improvements or changes are made.

- **Structure**
  - Check the straightness of the walls both internally and externally for any signs of cracking or movement.

  - Look for evidence of movement around window frames, doors and floor levels.

  - Beware of recently caulked and painted walls, or any areas externally which have new mortar.

- **Damp**
  - Check for signs of damp by removing floor surfaces to check underneath.

  - Peel off wallpaper to indicate any presence of damp.

  - Beware of any recent decoration which may have been completed to disguise any number of sins.

- **Dimensions**
  - Measure the rooms and check you can fit standard-size baths and appliances in the bathroom and kitchen. Smaller or larger items will attract a higher cost price.

- **Outside**
  - Check the outside space and take notes of any boundary lines such as fences and walls and whether any maintenance work is required.

- ○ Make notes of any parking arrangements, or where parking could be improved (such as lowering of the kerb to create off-street car parking).

- ○ Note down any pathways, roads and manholes that run close to the property, or are within the boundary.

- ○ Check if the neighbours have made any alterations to their properties (such as loft conversions, extensions) as a precedent may have been set for these alterations in the area.

- **Planning**
  - ○ Check the appropriate consents are in place. If any changes have been made to the property, ensure these have the required permissions or regulation approval.

Additional points if a property is leasehold:

- **Common areas**
  - ○ Check the condition of the communal areas and ensure you understand who is responsible for the upkeep.

  - ○ Investigate any areas of repair, or items which require improvement.

(Nick Dare MRICS, Dare Property Ltd)

Top surveyor tip

Talk to the neighbours. Ask them if they have any issues with the property – you'd be surprised how much people notice.

Turn detective: why is this property being sold at auction?

Properties are sold at auction for a reason. Your mission, should you choose to accept it, is to understand what those reasons are. Most properties are sold at auction because:

1. A quick sale is needed (for example, the property has been repossessed or the owner is in financial trouble and needs to raise funds quickly).

2. The property has structural problems or legal issues that would prevent it being sold easily on the open market (for example, the property requires work of a specialist nature to unlock its true market value).

3. The property is being sold by a public body, such as the council or the police, and an auction sale is necessary to prove the 'best price possible' is obtained in the public interest.

4. The property is located in an area where demand is low, is very price-sensitive and/or does not appeal to local homeowners.

5. The property is unique and difficult to value as there are no direct comparisons on the market (for example, a potential development site or a lighthouse situated on the beach front).

The key thing to remember with auction properties is that most of them *could* be sold by an estate agent and thus the most important question to ask – and to find the answer to – is: **why is this property being sold at auction?**

This question requires a very critical analysis of the property, which is not normally considered when conducting a viewing with an estate agent. When viewing an auction property you must always be on the lookout for potential problems. This is not the time to get starry-eyed and think about where the new sofa will go, or the sort of colour scheme which will match. This is the time to ask: what is wrong with this property?, why did this not sell with an estate agent?, what are the problems? The answers to these questions are not always immediately obvious, and in fact, even upon viewing, the issues may not become apparent – but do remember always to be suspicious and always ask: why?

Top questions to ask of a property being sold at auction

- Why is this property being sold at auction and not with an estate agent?
  - What are the reasons why this was not sold or could not be sold on the open market?

- Who is selling the property?
  - Is it a mortgagee in possession, a public body, a private individual?

- Why is this property being sold?
  - What is the motivation for selling the property at auction? Is it for a quick sale? An accountable sale? Because the property requires work or has legal issues?

Some of these questions may have been answered in your previous research. But it is best practice to reassess these answers when at the viewing to confirm your earlier find-ings. Never be afraid to ask questions of a property's history. When buying at auction – it is better to ask the questions while you can, because once the gavel has come down, it'll be too late!

LEGAL INSIGHT

The general view is that if a property is being sold at auction there must be something wrong with it in some way, otherwise it should be capable of being sold in the ordinary course by private treaty. In some cases this can be a misconception because there might be genuine reasons why a property is being sold in a public auction rather than by private treaty (for instance, the person selling the property needs a quick sale). As a good rule of thumb buyers should always be wary and extra vigilant when it comes to buying properties at public auction. Any person looking to buy a property at auction should firstly be asking himself (or herself) why has this property ended up in a public auction and why hasn't it already been sold in the ordinary course through an estate agent? (Michael John Hayward, solicitor)

Hone your detective skills – is this property trying to hide a secret?

At the property viewing it is important to assess the build-ing and carry out some 'sense checks'. Sense checks are about trying to uncover the secret life of a property and its previous occupants. You should look to undertake the following checks:

- Check for signs of life – when was the property last lived in or occupied?
  - How does the property smell – can you smell any signs of life, any indication of damp/mould?

○ What is the temperature in the property – when was the heating last used?

○ How long has the property been empty – is there any underlying reason for that?

○ Is there any further damage which may have been caused while the property has been vacant? (Look for water stain marks on the ceiling which may indicate a leak).

- Check the post – how recent are the postmarks on the mail? What sort of mail is it (for example, utility bills or debt collection letters)? How many addressees are receiving mail at the property address?

- Check for previous agency activity – are there any agency boards taken down? Are there any viewing lists from an estate agent? Is there any estate agency literature hidden anywhere?

- Check for any signs of recent maintenance works – has the property (or any area of it) recently been redecorated or replastered? Was this to improve the property for sale or to hide a structural defect? (Recently hung wallpaper is known to cover a multitude of sins!)

- Check all windows and doors open and close freely; a door that sticks may indicate a structural problem with the property.

- Check for anything that looks out of place (for example, a new window installation when all other windows in the building require replacement).

These sense checks do not take long on a viewing, and can add valuable insight to your property research. They can also raise important questions which may lead to further investigation.

AUCTIONEER INSIGHT

Properties can be put into auction as a first option to sell and also a last resort when every other method of sale has failed. Some are put into auction because they are difficult to sell or because there is something wrong with them (for example, legal or structural issues). Research is the key to understanding the sort of property and potential issues you may be taking on. (Guy Charrison, Network Auctions)

CASE STUDY: THE CAMBRIDGE SQUATTER IN THE BACK GARDEN

An auction property in Cambridge.

Auction property in Cambridge is very rare. With a strong local market and high demand, there is not enough housing stock to go around. So when a property in Cambridge was being sold at a London auction room there was much excitement. The property was a repossession and initial research looked promising. The viewing was scheduled for a weekday morning and upon arrival at the property there was already a group of some fifty people waiting to view.

The property appeared to have sound reasons for sale at auction – it was a repossession requiring work. However, it was unusual that the property should be sold at auction rather than through a local estate agent. The condition was mortgageable and there was plenty of buyer interest.

The property did not look as if it had been lived in for some time (as evidenced by the lack of post, and unkempt ivy growing into the windows); however, there did appear to be a new-looking fence at the rear of the property. This alerted my detective instincts: why was there a new-looking fence at this unlived-in property? This fence required further investigation.

TIP

You should always be looking for something that is out of place.

From the upstairs bedroom window (which was quite difficult to see out of because of the overgrown ivy) the location of the fence could be seen. What also could be seen, situated behind the fence, was a static caravan. Moreover, looking at the garden from the upstairs angle, it was visible that the garden belonging to the auction property was considerably smaller than the neighbouring gardens. This then raised several questions which required further detective work.

The detective work revealed the Cambridge property was indeed trying to hide a secret. It transpired that, prior to the property being repossessed, the former owner transferred part of the garden belonging to the property to a family relative. The lender, at that time, had allowed this transfer to happen. This meant part of the garden was now free of the lender's charge and they had no ownership of it: the garden was registered as a separate title with a different owner. When the property was repossessed, the former owner simply upped sticks and moved to the part of the garden which was not owned by the bank, installed a static caravan and erected a new fence. The former owner was able to access the garden, since a right of way across the former property had also been allowed as part of the earlier transfer. The council had been battling for years for the eviction and removal of the static caravan and the occupants, but because the former owners had nowhere to live or move to the judge had seen fit to allow the occupants and the caravan to remain. This meant any new purchaser would be buying the property with the former owners squatting in the back garden!

No viewings arranged

In certain cases, internal viewings are detailed as 'not available'. This may be for a number of reasons:

1. The property is tenanted and the auction house has been unable to contact the tenants, or the tenants have refused to cooperate.

2. The property is occupied by protected tenants.

3. The property is occupied under terms unknown.

4. The property is being sold by mortgagee not in possession.

5. The property is unsafe for internal viewing.

In the majority of these cases, the reason why viewings are not organised is because the property is currently tenanted. Under tenancy law tenants have a right to 'peaceful enjoyment' of the property. This means that if the tenants refuse entry this right must be respected. On some occasions tenants may be willing to show the property to prospective buyers, but this is at their discretion, rather than a right to which any new buyer is entitled.

If you approach a tenanted property, it is important to be understanding of the situation and also the rights to which tenants are entitled. Should you be fortunate enough to be allowed entry to a property by a tenant, this is an ideal time to find out as much as possible about the property and any issues and problems. Most tenants will give an honest appraisal of the property and can point out any issues which may have gone unnoticed at a normal viewing.

In the case of properties which are listed as 'unsafe' for internal viewing – these should only be checked externally. In some cases it may be possible to arrange with the auction house for a qualified surveyor to assess the property, but this is at their discretion and will depend upon the nature of the property risk. Auction houses go to great lengths to obtain access to properties which they are selling, and it is only in the most extreme cases where an internal viewing is classified as unsafe.

Insider Insight

Some auction houses will upload details to the major property websites such as Rightmove and Zoopla before the actual auction catalogue is produced or listed online. If you are looking for a property in a specific area, a search alert should be set up which will notify you of all new properties in the search area as soon as they are entered onto the system. This will give you a head start on potential properties being sold in your area of interest.

Chapter Summary

This chapter has looked at the key ways of finding and viewing auction property. Thousands of properties are sold at auction and it is critical to understand why a property is being sold at auction rather than through an estate agent. Auction catalogues are sales brochures and are designed to tempt buyers and also to ensure a successful sale day. Thorough research should be conducted prior to the viewing to ascertain key facts about the property. At the viewing it is necessary to act like a surveyor and a detective and investigate thoroughly the reasons for sale at auction. Some properties do not have organised viewings and, if tenanted, access will be at the discretion of the tenant.

Expert Tip

People can become very competitive at block viewings and may say negative things about the property or the area for the benefit of others at the viewing to hear – and be deterred by. It is important to undertake your own thorough research and feel comfortable with the property and the area rather than listening to hearsay.

Watch Point

Many people still think 'you can't go wrong with property' and buy properties from the catalogue on the basis of the photograph and particulars. This practice is incredibly risky and can be very expensive if a property is not as expected. Appearances can be deceptive and the external appearance of a property does not always bear any relation to the internal condition.

CHAPTER 5
Preparation is Key to Success

'Fail to prepare, prepare to fail.'
(Benjamin Franklin)

Buying property at auction requires scrupulous preparation to ensure future success. Unlike when buying property with an estate agent, when you offer (bid) to buy at auction, your bid is contractually binding through to sale completion. This means all research about the property needs to be conducted *before* bidding. This is the opposite way round from buying with an estate agent, where the offer is placed first and then the research is done last. With property at auction research comes first, then the offer comes last. The auction buying process is heavily front-loaded and it needs to be – once you've bought the property, *you've bought the property*! It is therefore key you have carried out all due diligence on a property before committing to buy at auction.

It may sound onerous, but the mantra 'believe nothing and check everything' should be rigorously applied when buying property at auction.

Every last detail must be checked, checked and checked again:

- Check what you are buying is what you *want* to be buying.

- Check what you think you are buying is what you are *actually* buying.

- Check what money you have is *enough* to buy what you want.

The key areas of preparation before buying an auction property are surveying the property, the legal conveyance and organising the finances.

To survey or not to survey?

People often have mixed views on property surveys. This is probably due to the fact most people's experiences of surveys have been limited to the condition report which is commissioned by a bank when applying for mortgage finance. This survey is insisted upon by the bank and is more accurately described as a 'mortgage valuation' than a property survey. This survey, which is conducted by a surveyor on behalf of the bank, is actually a report to the bank regarding the suitability of the property as security for the loan. The report may highlight some works which are required at the property, but the primary function is to check the property provides adequate security for the loan. The survey is not designed to assist the buyer of the property – it is actually to report to the lender on the suitability of the property as security for the loan. All lenders require a condition report to be carried out on a property before deciding to lend and this fee will be charged to you.

Property surveys which are carried out on behalf of the buyer are quite different from those which the bank instructs. Most importantly, when a buyer instructs a survey report, the findings are reported to them, on their behalf and for their own purpose, rather than the bank. This means the survey results can shed further light on the property and any potential issues which may arise, rather than the surveyor simply checking if the property is suitable security for the purpose of the bank loan.

Are surveyors worth the money?

Property surveys carried out by a qualified member of the Royal Institution of Chartered Surveyors (RICS) and commissioned by the buyer of a property can provide a wealth of information. Surveyors are expert assessors and are professionally trained to look for key building defects and any issues which may affect the value of the property now and in the future. RICS recognises three types of property survey:

- **Condition report.** The inspection is brief and the main aim of the report is to value the property on behalf of the lender to ensure it reflects the loan amount. The valuation is based on the surveyor's knowledge of comparable prices in the locality. It may also give a 'minimum reinstatement value' for insurance purposes, which is the amount of money it would take to rebuild the property from scratch, should it ever be necessary.

- **Homebuyer report.** The homebuyer report is suitable for conventional properties which are in a reasonable condition and built within the last 150 years. The report is fairly comprehensive and, in addition to a market valuation and insurance reinstatement figure, also details and gives advice on any defects that may affect the value of the property and recommendations for repairs and ongoing maintenance. This report can also cover any specific concerns which you would like the surveyor's opinion on.

- **Building survey.** A full structural survey is a comprehensive report providing detailed information about the fabric and condition of the property. The survey is particularly useful if the property is in poor condition, old, unusual, substantially altered or if you are planning any renovations or alterations to the property. The report will have a list of recommendations and provide advice on how to remedy any defects and maintenance issues. The surveyor may also be able to provide an estimate of repair costs and a valuation as separate services. If you require bank finance for the property, a valuation should be ordered in addition as this does not normally accompany the survey.

(Source: rics.org/uk)

The type of survey you instruct will depend upon the property, condition and your future plans for the building. It is worth noting that only a homebuyer guide and building survey are commissioned on behalf of the buyer. The condition report is primarily a report to the lender on the suitability of the property as security for the loan. It is advisable to commission a survey for your own requirements to ensure you understand the property fully before committing to buy.

TIP

To gain maximum value, the property survey should be instructed early in the process so that any findings or recommendations can be investigated further.

Typical survey fee costs

Survey costs vary according to the property, value and

location: at the time of writing, for an average £150,000 to £200,000 property, a homebuyer's survey cost between £300 and £420, and a building survey between £560 and £730. This is a significant outlay on a property which you do not own, but it is a small price to pay for being made aware of any expensive issues which you had not previously noticed. To save costs, it may be possible to combine the expense of the valuation report (which the lender will insist on) with the price of a homebuyer's survey. The other option could be to contact an independent RICS surveyor and request a verbal report on the property. This may consist of a meeting at the property and a verbal report while on site, or perhaps a telephone call after the visit. The verbal report option may help to reduce costs because the surveyor will not be required to spend a huge amount of time in completing a full written report. While it is difficult to justify spending so much money upfront, it is worth bearing in mind that a good surveyor is likely to save you money in the long term by highlighting any potential issues.

If you decide not to go down the surveyor route it is still advisable to obtain a professional opinion on the condition of the building.

Alternative to a surveyor: a trusted builder

A trusted builder will be able to help you assess the condition of the building and pinpoint works which need to be carried out and any future maintenance issues. When using a builder to evaluate a property, it is important to bear in mind that they have different skills from a surveyor and will provide a more practical perspective on the property. This can prove very useful when itemising and costing works, but it is also important to retain a holistic view of the property and not get bogged down in job specifics. You should be aware that a builder (even a trusted one) will usually have a vested interest in the property and will be hopeful that the site visit may lead to future work. Builders are not as impartial as surveyors – although they may be able to offer more practical advice and solutions.

Alternative to a surveyor and a trusted builder: a good friend!

If you do not have any contacts in the building trade and do not want the expense of a survey, it is at least advisable to get a second opinion from a friend. Second opinions from friends (even if you sometimes don't agree with them) are invaluable as a 'reality check'. When viewing auction property, especially those which have potential (such as requiring major works), it is very easy to get carried away and underestimate the costs required. While it is important to be optimistic and wear rose-tinted glasses, grand designs can sometimes get in the way of common sense and profit. Vision is required to unlock the potential of many auction properties; nevertheless, it is important to be realistic about timelines and budgets. A second pair of eyes (preferably from a friend who is constructively critical) will usually bring you down to earth and raise important questions for consideration.

The legal pack: be sure what you're buying is what you're buying

Caveat Emptor is the byword when buying property at auction. It is Latin for '*Let the buyer beware*'.

When buying property at auction the buyer should be aware and beware. Properties are sold at auction for a reason – it is essential that the legal paperwork associated with a property is checked thoroughly before bidding and committing to buying a property.

Every property which is sold at auction will have legal documentation which accompanies the sale particulars and is often referred to as 'the legals' or 'the legal pack'.

The usual contents of a legal pack for an auction property will have the following:

- Conditions of sale.

- Special conditions.

- Title deeds and title plan.

- Lease, plan and service charge information (if leasehold).

- EPC.

- Office copies.

- Local authority searches.

- Environmental search.

- Drainage and water search.

- Coal mining search (in certain geographic areas).

- Chancel check (if applicable).

- Tenancy agreement/ lease (if applicable).

The legal pack is generally available one to two weeks prior to the auction sale date. Usually, legal documents can be downloaded direct from the auction house website free of charge, although some auction houses may charge a nominal fee. Online access to the legal pack is the most cost- and time-effective way to access these documents. In some cases, the auction house may post legal documents and for this there is usually a set charge of around £15–£25. It is advisable for speed, cost and convenience to download legal documents where possible as these can be easily and instantly shared with your solicitor and any other third parties where necessary.

TIP

If any of the legal paperwork is missing or cannot be provided, you should proceed very carefully and only under the expert guidance of a qualified solicitor.

CASE STUDY: THE RENTED PROPERTY WHERE NO RENT WAS BEING PAID

We were interested in purchasing a purpose-built block of flats which was being sold by the receivers. The former owners, who had also built the block, had been made bankrupt and the court had ordered the sale of the property. The legal paperwork showed that all flats were currently rented at market rental value and deposits were being held by the landlord. The paperwork gave the impression that the property would make a good rental investment which would produce income from day one.

However, our solicitor was concerned because an up-to-date rental statement had not been provided. This statement would enable us to be sure the rents were being paid and payments were up to date. Despite several requests for this information from the sellers, this information was not provided.

Prior to the auction, and on account of some diligent digging, it was discovered that rent had not been received for some of the flats for over two years. While it was decided this non-receipt of rent was not sufficient to deter us from bidding for the property, it did enable us to plan correctly in terms of finance. Rents, which were expected to be received as income for the property, could no longer be taken into account, and, more importantly, an additional sum needed to be set aside to allow for the costs of evicting the non-paying tenants.

Study the basic legal paperwork yourself

At this point I am not suggesting you become a solicitor in a day! However, it is sensible to undertake an initial check on the legal paperwork to familiarise yourself with the property and any other matters which may arise. There are many basic property facts to be gleaned from the legal paperwork that will assist you in finding out more before you incur the expense of a solicitor.

As a minimum, the basic facts that you should look for in the legal paperwork are:

- **Title plan and title deeds (freehold):** Does the title include all that you thought you were buying? For example, is the garden size as you expected? Is the footprint of the property as you anticipated? Are there any unexpected rights of ways or covenants on the building? Have any of the boundaries been changed? Has any of the property been sold off on different titles?

- **Title plan and title deeds (leasehold):** Is the length of the lease long enough (remember the eighty-year rule – less than eighty years and it will cost you to extend the lease)? Is the annual ground rent an acceptable amount? Do the service charge costs look reasonable? Are there any major works planned at the property, and if so, is there any indication regarding costs? Is the plan of the property as you expected? Is there an active management company? Is there a freeholder present? Have the last three years' service charge accounts been included?

- **Office copies and local searches:** Is the property located within a conservation area? Are there any planning permissions on file? Building regulation notices? Are there any planned works in the area or any designated urban changes which may be approved? Is the property connected to mains water/sewerage system?

- **Special conditions:** Is there anything unusual, such as completion within fourteen days, 10 per cent deposit cleared funds to bid, sellers' contribution to legal expenses (this is common with many local authority disposals who sometimes charge up to 3 per cent of the property value as a contribution)? Is VAT to be added? Is it only to be sold to owner-occupiers? Are there any clawback conditions (quite a common occurrence with land being sold at auction)?

- **Tenant information** (if occupied): Is there proof of current rent payments? Are deposits held and where are they lodged? (As the new owner and landlord you will become liable for any deposits.) Is there a current assured shorthold tenancy (AST) and are the details correct? Is the current rent a market rent? (Check for over-inflated rents and unrealistic yields.) Is it a Regulated Tenancy? (These types of tenanted property are common at auction and are protected by law. Regulated tenancies are very different to assured shorthold tenancies and require specialist knowledge before purchasing.)

- **Energy Performance Certificate (EPC):** This will enable you to check the size and energy performance-related features of the property. Does the property have wall, roof and floor insulation and how can this be improved? What is the heating and hot water supply to the property? What condition are the windows in and what lighting is currently used? The EPC will also provide recommended measures to improve the energy rating of the property with indicative costs and savings per year.

Studying the legal pack at an early stage will provide you with a comprehensive overview of the property to make an informed decision.

AUCTIONEER INSIGHT

The special conditions are the key document in the legal pack as it is within these conditions where a lot of the 'naughties' as I call them, are contained. This document sets out some of the key items which a buyer should be made aware of. For example, many local authorities charge an additional premium to the buyer of between 1 and 3 per cent of the hammer price as a contribution towards their costs of selling at auction. (Guy Charrison, Network Auctions)

Get a solicitor to double-check

It can seem very expensive to request a solicitor to check the legals prior to bidding on a property at auction – after all, you have no guarantee that you will be successful. However, buying a property which later transpires to have legal issues is ultimately much more expensive than the initial cost of having a solicitor double-check the documents.

Most good solicitors understand the requirements for speed when buying a property at auction. They are well versed in the tricks of the trade and know exactly what they are looking for in the auction paperwork. In comparison to an estate agent sale where the conveyance may take several weeks, a good solicitor will usually be able to provide an informed opinion within a couple of days. The legal pack is likely to contain the majority of the information they require. However, if, for any reason, a document is missing, the solicitors may be able to request this prior to auction. The typical charge for checking legal paperwork before auction is approximately £150–£350 plus VAT. If you are successful at auction, it is common practice to complete the sale with the same solicitor who undertook the initial legal work on the property. Generally, a discount is applied to the final legal price, in view of the fees already paid for the work prior to auction.

Auction property can occasionally have legal issues which affect the property and, in some cases, may have an impact upon the ability to raise finance. Legal property problems are often the most expensive to resolve and can cause the most amount of headaches. Many of these issues cannot even be seen by the naked eye. However, their importance must not be underestimated. Legal property problems can have a hugely detrimental effect on the value – and can cost far more to rectify than any proposed refurbishment might.

The main legal issues that could have an impact upon the ability to raise finance on a property are:

- Defective lease clause(s).

- Absentee freeholder or no management company.

- No planning permission or building regulations.

- No right of way.

- No defined access.

- Incorrect/unregistered/complicated title deeds and/or plans.

- Land Registry charges.

- Environmental charges.

- Non-standard construction.

- Former mining area (the presence of a mine shaft).

These issues are problematic as they mean the property may not be deemed as suitable security for a loan. Every property is different, and so it is always worth taking expert legal advice before proceeding.

LEGAL INSIGHT

Most firms of solicitors will carry out a check of the auction property legal pack and report to prospective bidders prior to auction for a reasonable fee. This is especially important if the title to the property is unregistered or, if it is registered, it has a complicated title. Also, if it's a repossession sale or a sale by receivers on behalf of a registered charge holder, this needs looking into further. (Michael John Hayward, solicitor)

TIP

Ensure you understand all of the contractual and legal conditions which relate to buying property at auction. If in doubt – ask!

CASE STUDY: THE FLAT WITH NO RIGHT OF ACCESS TO ENTER

Property in London is usually any auction house's best seller and sale prices reach far in excess of the guide price due to the demand for people wanting to own property in the capital. Thus I noted with surprise that a repossessed one-bedroom flat in Brixton with a guide price of £100,000 did not sell. The reserve price was £100,000 and the flat was available to buy after auction. Research of the local area suggested the flat had a resale price with an estate agent of £175,000. This appeared to be too good an opportunity to miss!

A brief perusal of the legals showed the lease had in excess of 100 years, there was a management company and freeholder, the service charge accounts looked reasonable and the ground rent was a nominal £50 per year. The flat had planning permission and building regulations and the EPC showed the flat to be a good size. On paper it all looked very promising, so a viewing was booked.

The flat was in dated decorative order, but the refurbishment was mainly cosmetic and would cost approximately £10,000 to leverage the potential. With a reserve price of £100,000, a budget of £10,000 and a potential resale of £175,000 the flat looked like a gold mine! But something did not feel right. This was just too good to be true – why did this flat not sell with an estate agent, nor sell at the auction room? I was desperate to make an offer and secure the deal before anybody else spotted the potential, but I knew that something was amiss with the deal. I just couldn't put my finger on it.

The legal documents were sent to my solicitor who dug deeper and the problems with the bargain Brixton flat came to light: the flat had no legal right of access! The flat was situated in a building which had been converted approximately twenty-five years ago. To enter the flat, which was on the first floor, access was required via the communal hallway and stairs. However, for some reason (most likely an error in the lease) no right of way over the communal parts had been given to the flat – which meant it was land-locked! The only way to 'unlock' the flat would be to apply to the freeholder for a variance of the lease (and there was no guarantee they would agree), but more importantly, the freeholder could charge a premium for granting access to the flat. The major issue was that the cost of the premium was unknown – meaning you could end up being held ransom to enter your own flat. The unknown costs and potential issues involved in the purchase made this an incredibly risky buy. This then explained why the flat had not sold with an estate agent, nor sold in the auction room. Of course, the legal issue could probably be resolved, but it was a risk I was not willing to take.

Raising the finance: have the 'readies' ready!

When buying property at auction it is paramount you have the funds available – or at least access to the funds – should you make a successful bid. On auction day you will exchange immediately and a 10 per cent deposit will become due and payable to the auctioneer. This must be paid by cheque, debit card or banker's draft. These must be cleared funds. Once you have exchanged, the balance of the funds will usually become due twenty-eight days later, although it has become increasingly common for completion to take place within fourteen days on many repossessed properties. This is an incredibly short amount of time to raise finance given the paperwork involved – and given the difficulty there is in trying to obtain mortgage finance quickly. Bearing in mind the strict time deadlines, it is advisable to have funding in place prior to bidding at auction and to ensure any lender is aware of the property being an auction purchase and the completion deadline.

Failure to complete in time is a very serious matter. The sale agreement is a legally binding contract: should you not complete the sale you will forfeit the 10 per cent deposit and potentially be liable for legal action. Any delay on the completion date will also result in fines and penalties being levied on a daily basis – and these can soon mount up. Any delay to complete is best avoided at all costs.

LEGAL INSIGHT

The most frequent mistake I have seen from people buying at auction is that they haven't made sufficient arrangements to sort out their funding before bidding for the property. In most auctions, the buyer only has a period of twenty-eight days from the date of the auction to complete the contract and pay the remainder of the purchase money to the seller. In fact, in some auction sales, I have seen completion dates reduced to a period of only seven or fourteen days which makes things extremely tight. Even if a buyer believes they already have their mortgage finance 'approved in principle' with their lender, getting this sorted in time with their chosen lender is a constant struggle. Buyers should always have a 'Plan B' available (just in case the mortgage lender is unable to release the mortgage advance in time for completion). (Michael John Hayward, solicitor)

How to finance auction property

There are a variety of ways to finance buying a property at auction. We will look at the main finance options available.

Mortgage

It is a commonly held myth that mortgages are not available for purchasing auction properties. But mortgages *can* be used to buy property at auction – however the lender must be aware of the deadline and be able to act within the timeframe available. When using a mortgage to buy a property at auction, it is advisable for the mortgage agreement (this is often known as a 'decision in principle') to be in place before attending the auction to bid. This will require you to submit a mortgage application prior to auction and ensure the survey has been conducted and the lender is willing to lend on the property. This applies to all mortgages whether they are for residential home occupiers or buy-to-let investors.

Mortgage companies, contrary to popular belief, are willing to lend on properties which require some refurbishment works, and there are some specialist mortgage products on the market. The acid test in most cases is whether the property is habitable – that is, the property must have a kitchen sink and a toilet. Thus, while the property may require a new kitchen, bathroom, central heating, rewiring and a whole host of other upgrades – this does not necessarily mean a mortgage lender will not lend. The key test is whether the property is considered suitable security for the loan. This can only be assessed by a surveyor carrying out a valuation. Once the report has been received by the lender they will be in a position to make a decision. If you require mortgage funds to purchase a property, it is strongly advised this offer is in place before bidding at auction.

> ### *TIP*
> A kitchen sink and toilet are prerequisites to obtaining mort-gage finance.

Commercial Lending

Commercial lending is the term used for business bank loans. Commercial lending is a popular way to purchase property at auction due to the flexibility of such loans. Commercial lending can be placed on the property purchased at auction, or it can be charged against a different asset owned by the borrower. This allows the borrower to 'drawdown' funds to purchase a property, but does not necessarily mean the loan is secured on the property bought. If a property is to be secured via commercial lending, the bank will require a 'business case' for the loan which will show the financial viability of the property. Commercial lending usually requires the borrower to have experience and a strong track record before a line of finance will be considered.

Bridging

Bridging finance is a type of short-term loan which is generally used as an interim loan before the arrangement of larger or longer-term financing; hence the term 'bridge'. Bridging loans on a property are typically paid back when the property is sold or refinanced with a traditional lender. Bridging tends to be more expensive than traditional loans and mortgages, but they are usually arranged quickly and with relatively little documentation. Loans can be open (with no set date for payback of loan) or closed (with a set date for the exit of bridging finance).

Cash

Cash is the ultimate way to buy property at auction and gives the buyer enormous freedom and flexibility. As a cash buyer you are also afforded a wider range of opportunities which many banks and mortgage lenders would not consider. This means different risks can be taken and potentially higher rewards can be gained from the properties available at auction. However, it is not easy to raise such large quantities of cash and it is fairly common for investors or developers to club together to purchase at auction.

Auctioneer Insight

The financing of auction property has been, and still remains, a barrier for most people to purchase. However, this is starting to change and we are now seeing some vendors extending their completion dates to six weeks. This longer completion time allows an increasing number of people who need to organise finance to consider auction as a place where they can buy property. (Guy Charrison, Network Auctions)

Insider Insight

Preparing to buy a property at auction requires professional expertise in many areas. It is advisable to build a 'dream team' of trusted experts to call upon when looking to purchase property at auction.

Chapter Summary

This chapter has considered the key preparation necessary to buying a property at auction. It is essential that thorough research is conducted prior to bidding. A property survey will need to be undertaken if mortgage finance is required and it is advisable this is carried out before bidding. It is very easy to get carried away when a property requires works and it is preferable for a surveyor to be instructed, or a builder to attend to cost the works required. Property sold at auction can sometimes have legal issues and a solicitor should inspect the legal pack to ensure all queries are answered. Raising finance in the tight timeframe required is very difficult and should be organised before attending the auction. Property at auction can be bought with various finance methods, although cash is king.

Expert Tip

If a property sounds too good to be true, it usually is. Meticulous due diligence is required to ensure the property will make a solid investment.

Watch Point

Most legal documents relating to a property should be present in the legal pack. However, it is not unheard of for particular documents to be missing from the pack – this can happen by accident and also on purpose. Due diligence of all paperwork is essential to be sure of the property particulars. A good solicitor is well versed in these matters and should be consulted prior to any auction purchase.

CHAPTER 6
Calculating the Bid Price of a Property

'Making money out of property isn't rocket science – it's a numbers game.
You've just got to make sure the numbers are stacked in your favour!'

(Peter, property buyer)

Making money from property is a very simple mathematical sum: it is simply selling it for more than you bought it for plus any expenditure incurred. The trick is not to spend more than the property is worth – and that is a science!

Not every property that requires refurbishment or TLC will be a profitable venture or financially viable. In fact, it is often the case that some of the better presented properties at auction make the best buys. This is because so many people are attracted to the 'doer-uppers' – they overlook those properties which are 'ready to go', meaning there is less competition and potentially a lower price is paid. In the heat of the moment, and with the desire to put your own stamp on a property, it is easy for costs to get overlooked and the finer details of the financing to be forgotten. It is also fair to say that some people also brush off such details as minor details that are not so important to the overall end result of the project. Details, hidden costs and forgotten financial obligations can mount up surprisingly quickly – and seem to have a habit of doing so when every other anticipated cost also flies out of the window. It is therefore important to always have a handle on the budget and be aware of when you may be tricking yourself into believing 'it will be all right on the night'. Every cost, charge and expense needs to be accounted for to understand whether a property purchase will be profitable.

Hidden buying costs

The price you pay for a property at auction is just the start of a long list of expenses which will be added to the register of costs that will be incurred – and which will rapidly mount up. There are many hidden costs to buying a property besides the price paid at auction and any anticipated refurbishment costs. These hidden costs will often include:

- **Stamp Duty Land Tax (SDLT).** This is a tax which is charged on land and property transactions in the UK and is payable upon sale completion. The tax is charged at different thresholds and rates for different types of property and values of transaction. SDLT bands are subject to change, but the current residential land or property SDLT rates and thresholds as of January 2013 are:

    ○ 0 per cent up to £125,000.

    ○ 1 per cent over £125,000 to £250,000.

    ○ 3 per cent over £250,000 to £500,000.

    ○ 4 per cent over £500,000 to £1 million.

    ○ 5 per cent over £1 million to £2 million.

    ○ 7 per cent over £2 million.

    ○ 15 per cent over £2 million (purchased by certain persons including corporate bodies).

(Source: HM Revenue & Customs, 2013)

- **Buyer's premium.** When buying a property at auction, there is a fee which is payable by the buyer to the auction house. This may be known in various guises such as an 'administration fee' or 'auction house fee'. The amount of the buyer's premium varies between auction houses and can be a set fee ranging from £150 to £750, or may be calculated as a proportion of the property value, such as 1 per cent, or 2 per cent of the hammer price paid.

- **Legals.** The cost of the conveyancing work will vary according to the value of the property and the amount of work which is required. Typically a leasehold property will cost more in legal fees than a freehold property because the solicitor will have to spend more time inspecting a lease. In addition to the solicitor's fees there are also various disbursements which need to be paid and which will be added to the final bill along with VAT. In some cases, the seller of the property may demand a payment towards legal paperwork provided (for example, the reimbursement of local searches) or even a contribution to their legal costs (perhaps 1 per cent of the sale price). This can rapidly escalate the bill. Moreover, any legal issues that need to be resolved will also quickly mount up to a considerable sum.

- **Finance costs.** The cost of raising finance to purchase a property can have many additional expenses involved besides the monthly or final interest paid on the money borrowed. This can include the initial loan arrangement fee, an administration fee, a security fee and a redemption fee along with a whole host of other charges which get added to the loan. It is vital that the small print of any loan agreement is checked carefully to ensure all charges are included in the total cost for finance – including the loan itself.

- **Survey.** The cost of the survey, whether organised by the lender for a mortgage valuation or for your own purposes, will add up to several hundreds of pounds and this needs to be accounted for.

- **Insurance.** Property bought at auction will usually need to be insured from the day of exchange. If the property is empty and uninhabited this policy will usually only provide minimal insurance cover and will attract a higher premium because of non-occupation. Any works that will be undertaken at the property should be communicated to the insurers and it may be necessary to add employer's liability to the policy. Leasehold property may benefit from insurance under the freeholder policy: check if cover is included.

These hidden costs need to be considered and added to the cost of buying when calculating the bid price of an auction property.

Calculating the price to pay: what is the property worth?

Obtaining an accurate valuation of the property is key to calculating the price which should be paid at auction. There are two values:

1. The value of the property in its current condition.

2. The end value of the property once works are complete.

It is important to understand both of these values so that the margin – the difference between the value of the property in its current condition and the value of the property in the future – can be correctly assessed. This margin will be the budget within which you will need to undertake any refurbishment works and resolve any issues, and also from where you will take your anticipated profit. It is critical to ensure there is enough margin to work with when buying property at auction to ensure you do not leave yourself out of pocket when the project is complete.

The key way to ensuring a profitable project is to research the market and understand comparable property values to make an accurate assessment of the property you intend to purchase.

Research the property market

There are plenty of free online tools which can be used to research the property market. The main way to value the price of a property, both current and future, is by the use of comparisons. This, in effect, means finding comparable properties and understanding the value of these in comparison to the property you are intending to buy. Obviously, not every property is the same, and thus any differences need to be allowed for and the value adjusted accordingly. The major property websites offer a wealth of information on available properties and most will provide measurements, descriptions and internal photographs.

TIP

An asking price for a property is not the same as the sold price for a property.

- **Rightmove** is the big daddy of the property listings world and offers the most comprehensive listings of all properties for sale and rent in the UK. They also have some very useful tools such as the 'Price Comparison Report' where you can see sold prices, and often this will include the property's original full listing with photos, floor plans and more details. See www.rightmove.co.uk

- **Property-Bee** is a clever Firefox add-on to Rightmove which can turbo-charge the results. The Property-Bee toolbar will show all changes to the price and details since the property was listed. This means you have a complete history of when the property was put on the market, price changes (up and down), whether the property has been sold subject to contract (SSTC) and come back onto the market, and any changes to the details. See www.property-bee.com

- **Zoopla** is another leading UK property website which offers a huge number of properties for sale and rent. Similarly to Rightmove, Zoopla lets you match up sold prices with old property listings, including pictures, asking prices, descriptions and floor plans. You can also obtain a ballpark valuation of a property (although this is very ball park!) based on previous sale prices in the area and market climate. See www.zoopla.co.uk

- **Nethouseprices** list all the actual sold prices of property from the Land Registry and the Registers of Scotland. Newly sold properties appear in the searches two to three months after the deal is done. This tool will allow you to research what price was previously paid for the property and what the actual sold prices are for properties in the area. Sold prices are provided by house number, street address and postcode but do not disclose actual property details, such as the number of bedrooms or condition of the property. This needs to be factored in when using the tool for house price comparisons. See www.nethouseprices.com

- **Our Property** also shows data from the Land Registry, but the search records go back further than those on Nethouseprices to 1995. They also have a useful house statistics tool whereby you can search for the most expensive, least expensive and most transient street in an area. See www.ourproperty.co.uk

- **Mouseprice** provides property sold prices and uses a 'heat map' to colour code average sold prices in an area ranging from red-hot to chilly. You can also obtain a basic valuation of a property by entering the postcode and number of bedrooms and Mouseprice will provide a broad range of values. Monthly email alerts can be set for chosen areas, including house sale price information and where sellers have dropped asking prices. Individual properties can also be tracked so that you are alerted when a property is bought, sold or the seller cuts the price. See www.mouseprice.com

- **Property Price Advice** provides a basic online valuation of a property. You are required to answer some simple questions and provide an email address. An upper and lower value for the property is provided, as well as the option to download a PDF guide which includes local schools and doctors. See www.propertypriceadvice.co.uk

- **PropertySnake** allows you to track falling property prices and shows which properties in an area have recently dropped their asking prices and by how much. Simply type in a postcode to display which properties have been reduced and the percentage the price has been cut. See www.propertysnake.co.uk

Property Price Trends

Average property prices can also provide a useful insight to the market trends in an area. Do bear in mind, though, that they are just averages and so individual values for a property will vary considerably depending upon the particular property type and area.

- **House Price Index,** based upon the official data of real sales from the Land Registry, gives average house prices by region and breaks them down into different property types. There is usually a time lag of three months on the data provided. See www.landregistry.gov.uk/ public/house-prices-and-sales

- **Registers of Scotland** is the Scottish equivalent of the Land Registry and provides sale volumes and average house prices by district with graphs plotting monthly average prices. There is usually a three-month time lag on the data recorded. See www.ros.gov.uk

- **Halifax's** housing research is based on mortgage approvals and updates faster than the Land Registry. Its official House Price Index features a regional house price map and average prices by postcode. See www. lloydsbankinggroup.com/media1/economic_insight/ halifax_house_price_index_page.asp

- **Nationwide** also provide a House Price Index which can give another perspective on the state of the housing market. The site allows you to download national and regional house price data, as well as more detailed analysis. See www.nationwide.co.uk/hpi/default.htm

- **HousePriceCrash** is a website with a pro-property price crash agenda; this aside, the site collects statistics from the Land Registry, *Financial Times* and Hometrack to display house price trends. In addition, the site tracks house price predictions from different experts to give an idea of what the future may hold. See www.housepricecrash.co.uk

These online property resources provide a good foundation for understanding local market trends and calculating the value of a property. While it is possible to formulate a valuation of the property online, it is still advisable to gauge the opinion of a local estate agent.

TIP
Online valuation tools and assessing comparable properties will provide you with a valuation range for the property.

Ask the estate agent

Estate agents regularly feature near the top of most-hated professions surveys in the UK; yet a good estate agent who has local knowledge is worth their weight in gold. It is also useful to bear in mind that later in the project you may require the services of an estate agent to sell or rent the finished property, and so it is good to start making connections with potential agents early on.

The key areas you need to understand are:

- Current demand in the local market.
  - What is driving this (for example, transport links, particular employers in the area, amenities, schools)?

- Current demand for this property type.
  - What sort of properties are people currently buying? Is there an influx of first-time buyers, investors or families who are buying particular housing stock?

- Current sales time and asking prices.
  - How long does it typically take to sell property? How close to asking price are properties achieving?

- Any recent or predicted changes in the buying population, or the sort of housing stock they are looking for.
  - A new transport link can start to change the profile of an area and attract different buyers looking for different housing stock.

- Thoughts and opinions about the local market – hopes and fears for the future.
  - Understand the local drivers of an area – what is motivating people to buy and also what are the barriers to buying in the area?

In addition to these questions about the local market, it is useful to choose a current property for sale with the estate agent that is comparable to the property under consideration. With a specific property to use as a conversation piece, an estate agent will be able to provide key insights that will enable you to better value your property in its present condition and what it may be worth in the future. Areas of discussion which may prove fruitful could include:

- Size of the property.
  - How much does an extra bedroom, bathroom, or bigger living room add to the value of a property?

- Condition of the property.
  - How modern or dated is it?
  - How much additional value can be gained by undertaking particular works and to what specification or level of finish?

- Length of lease.
  - What is the 'magic number' which has maximum value? What is the lease length at which the property will struggle to sell?

- Access to outside space or size of garden.
  - Is there a particular size or feature that influences the value?

- Parking facilities.
  - How does this impact upon the property value or saleability? What are the key parking arrangements to consider?

- Proximity to transport/town/schools/major employers.
  - How close does the property need to be to benefit from a price increase?

- Period features/ex-council.
  - What is the price premium (if any) for character features?
  - How much reduction (if any) should be applied if it is a purpose-built/ex-council property?

- Potential.
  - What desires do buyers have which they would be prepared to pay a premium for? Perhaps a top-of-the-range wet room, a large high-specification kitchen/diner or space for a home office/study?

Estate agents can provide a huge amount of information on the local property market, the buying and selling dynamics, the profile of the population and the key motivations and barriers in the market place. They are also well placed to identify areas where value can be added to a property and even specify the nature of works which buyers demand. Detailed research and analysis needs to be undertaken to accurately assess the future value of a property and identify the potential for opportunities to improve the end value. Comparison property details, sold price statistics and research undertaken via estate agents should form the basis of any calculation of the current and future value. This needs to be combined with local area research which can have a major impact on the value of a property now and in the future.

CASE STUDY: A TOP END KITCHEN OR A NEW BOILER?

We bought a property at auction which required refurbishment. The budget to complete the works was very tight – and became even tighter when it was discovered that all of the electrics needed rewiring. The property benefited from gas central heating, but it was a dated system using a back boiler rather than a modern boiler.

The kitchen also required replacing and as the room was a spacious kitchen/diner we had opted for a designer finish to appeal to a more premium audience. However, the budget would not stretch to *both* the designer kitchen and a new boiler.

We arranged for several estate agents to attend the property and sought their expert advice. All agents agreed that as long as the gas central heating system was in working condition and could be shown to be safe and operational, the designer kitchen would add more value to the property rather than a lower specification kitchen and a new boiler. A Gas Safe-registered engineer certified the gas central heating system and the designer kitchen was installed. The high-end kitchen became the key selling point of the property, which was successfully sold at the full asking price.

TIP

Be cost effective in refurbishment works. It is very easy to try to fix everything, but this is not always required. Add value in areas that are valued.

Local area knowledge

Location, location, location . . .

The location of a property ultimately underpins the value both now and in the future. There are multiple possibilities to change the internal look (and in some cases, the external look) of a property, but there are no possibilities to change its location. You have very little control over the street and the area in which the property is located, and thus it is vital you understand the local area in which the property stands.

There are various online resources which can be used to gather evidence about the local area. These should be combined with a good dollop of offline research – that is, walking the actual streets and locality of the property.

- **Neighbourhood profile.** UKLocalArea allows you to type in a postcode and it will generate a neighbourhood profile, listing everything from age to employment rates to education. You can also see the distance to the nearest railway station or assess local school performance. See www.uklocalarea.com

- **Neighbourhood statistics.** The government's site provides an array of statistics for serious number crunching on everything from poverty to access to services. The language can be quite jargon-heavy, but it provides a wealth of information on everything from average life expectancy, to the number of people who went bankrupt to the number of house fires. See www.neighbourhood.statistics.gov.uk

- **Crime.** The police crime-mapping website for England and Wales is a useful tool to understand crime in the area. It breaks down recorded crimes by street (for example, burglary, robbery and anti-social behaviour). This statistical analysis allows you to understand an area on a micro level and the patterns of crime in an area. See www.police.uk

- **Transport links.** The transport connections of an area can have a major impact on a property value. New transport links could add thousands to the price of property – although if they are located too close they could have a detrimental effect. The Highways Agency road project search enables you to look for new roads in England (see www.highways.gov.uk/roads). For properties in London, www.commutefrom.com is a website which allows you to search, by tube station and journey length, the best commuter routes to office locations. It is also worth researching the new Cross Rail routes planned in and around London because these could have an enormous impact on the future value of property in these locations.

- **Schools.** The standard of education in an area can have a major impact on the value of the property. Inspection reports for primary and secondary schools in a particular postcode area can be searched on the Ofsted website. See www.ofsted.gov.uk/inspection-reports/find-inspection-report. The Department for Education also produce school league tables (see www.education.gov.uk/schools/performance/archive/index.shtml).

- **Local plans.** Planning applications in the local area could have an impact on the value of the property. The government's Planning Portal allows you to search, by postcode and area, for any planning applications made. See www.planningportal.gov.uk/inyourarea

- **Local environment.** Environmental hazards, such as risk of flooding, can influence the value of a property. Homecheck collates data from bodies like the Environment Agency and the British Geological Survey to analyse the risk of flooding, subsidence and other environmental problems, such as landfill waste and radon gas levels (see www.homecheck.co.uk). Further checks can be made direct with the Environment Agency which provides detailed reports on flood information and an air quality map showing nearby pollution dangers such as sewerage works. For England and Wales see www.environment-agency.gov.uk/homeandleisure/floods/default.aspx, and for Scotland see www.sepa.org.uk/default.aspx. For some cities in England, you can also track road traffic noise. See http://services.defra.gov.uk/wps/portal/noise.

Undertaking thorough research of the area will enable you to consider how local factors may affect the current and future value of a property.

The next stage requires you to cost the refurbishment programme to enable you to hone your bid price further.

Cost the works of the property

Accurately calculating the costs of works is vital to ensuring the project is successful – and profitable. Every refurbishment project is different – even if on the surface they look similar. Different properties have had different owners, different occupants, different histories and different things which have gone wrong over the years. Some properties may have been better looked after than others, some may have taken more wear and tear, and others may have been exploited – or simply abandoned. Your job, when taking on a property refurbishment project, is to fix all these problems – to condemn them to history. Your role in the story of the property is to give it a new start, a new lease of life and create a happy ending. This costs money and takes time. This needs to be calculated from the outset to ensure you and the property, find a happy ending.

Plan the works

To calculate the costs of a project, you will need a plan. You will need to know now, what you intend to do in the future. If you want to change the current bedroom in the property to become a kitchen instead, then this needs to be planned. If you intend to change the bathroom suite, build an extension, or even simply redecorate, all of these works need to be planned so they can be accurately costed. Without a plan you cannot cost works. It is also worth bearing in mind that although plans can be changed, once work has commenced changes to the original plan become more expensive, time-consuming – and in some cases cannot be implemented without major upheaval. It is therefore paramount that you spend a great deal of time at the start of the project thinking about, preparing and planning the works. If you have commissioned a survey report, any findings should also be included at this stage.

When planning a renovation project it's important to decide how far you want to go with it. This means thinking about and envisaging what the finished project will look like – and the level of work and detail you are prepared to go to. It may be you plan to own the property for a number of years either as your own home or as an investment, and thus how you approach the project and how far you go with it may have a different answer than if you were renovating the project for a quick sale to a third party. Even as an investment property, this plan will also vary according to the value of the property, the anticipated end user and the predicted rental premium. As a rule of thumb with property renovations, you should always bear in mind the 'ceiling price' (top price) of the property in the local market, rather than renovating the property to your own personal tastes and standards. This rule can be relaxed a little if the property is intended to be a long-term family home, although it is never wise to overspend on a property to the extent that your outlay is more than it could be worth when the works are complete.

TIP

Always bear in mind the ceiling price of a property, these ceilings are very hard to smash, no matter how great the finish!

Another important part of the planning of a project is to work out how you can best add value to a property. In some cases this may be fairly straightforward and require the updating of kitchen and bathroom fittings or the installation of gas central heating, upgrading of electrics and so forth. On other projects, it may be that the property would benefit from an internal rearrangement to improve the flow of the property or perhaps even the addition of an extension or a loft conversion. Some projects may even have the potential to create additional dwellings via sub-division, extensions, or new dwellings within the boundaries.

In all of these cases, it is vital you pay attention to the costs of the works and the actual value which they will add to the end value. There is no point spending £20,000 on a loft conversion if it only adds £15,000 to the end value of the property. A good rule of thumb to follow is that the value added should be at least *double* the cost of the works. Thus, if it costs £1,000 to install a new kitchen, you should anticipate the new kitchen adds at least £2,000 to the end value of the property. It is also important to note that some works do not add value to a property per se, but they do make the property more saleable. While it is more difficult to quantify the value of these works, it is essential that the costs and end value are calculated to ensure the works are worthwhile.

TIP

As a general guide, the value added to a property should be at least double the cost of the works.

Schedule of works

Once you have a plan in place and you know what you want to do to the property, what it will look like, how far you want to go and how you can best add value, it is time to prepare a schedule of works. A schedule of works is basically a shopping list of what you plan to do to the property so that contractors are able to quote on the project. The beauty of having a shopping list is that it is very easy to compare and contrast builders' quotes and to identify any areas of unusual expense. Many property developers and investors use Microsoft Excel to write their shopping list, which easily allows you to list each item and the builder to provide you with the costs next to the item. The total can be easily tallied at the end, but it is also simple to make any adjustments to the sums if required. There are many professional software packages available on the market – but Excel is a good, universally accepted programme for this sort of work.

Below is an example of a schedule of works which I used when I required builders' quotes for works to the roof, front elevation and windows on a property. You will see the shopping list is quite specific in terms of the materials used. This tight specification meant the builders were clear on what they were pricing for and thus I was able to compare quotes on a like-for-like basis. This is very important because you need to be sure you are comparing apples with apples and not apples with pears!

In the sample below, you will see that I specifically instructed the type of glazing to be used, the replacement of the guttering in cast iron, and the retiling of the roof in 50 per cent reclaimed tiles and 50 per cent salvaged from the existing roof. In this schedule of works, I also included a provisional contingency sum to allow for any unforeseen problems when retiling the roof. The reason for this inclusion was to put all builders on an equal footing – that is, if the provisional sum had *not* been included, then some builders may have requested a different allowance for unforeseen roofing repairs. This would have made direct comparisons of the quotes more difficult. The more specific and tight a schedule of works is, the more accurate the quote for the works will actually be – meaning there is less risk of any nasty surprises at the end of the project.

Schedule of works: roof, windows & front external	£
NB. architect will provide drawings of the windows specification and front elevation	
Hack off and rerender (in LIME) to the front elevation within heritage design scope	
Removal of the step detail to the front elevation and making good to receive render	
Replace 2 x no windows to the front elevation to match surrounding heritage designs (and neighbouring property) using SLIMLITE glazing	
1st floor window using SLIMLITE glazing	
2nd floor window using SLIMLITE glazing	
Replace 2 x windows, 1 door and frame and 1 vestibule door and frame to the rear of the property using SLIMLITE glazing	
1st floor window using SLIMLITE glazing	
Door with vestibule frame using SLIMLITE glazing	
Higher ground floor window using SLIMLITE glazing	
Door and frame to higher ground floor using SLIMLITE glazing	
Replacement of guttering in CAST IRON to front and rear elevation including fascia boards to comply with heritage design	
Include new downspouts front and rear	
To strip the existing roof to the front and rear elevations, supply and fit new breathable felt, treated timber batten and retile with 50 per cent reclaimed, 50 per cent salvaged from existing roof, new lead flashings to all existing chimneys	
Scaffolding to front and rear of property with a pavement permit to facilitate removal and fitting of windows, rendering, guttering and roofing	

Decorations to all new windows, doors and frames, existing front and bars, new render and all fascias, soffits, gutters and downspouts	
Replace 4 x (quantity) 250x380mm panels of glass in ground floor front using SLIMLITE glazing	
Take down wall behind render below 1st floor window and any existing signage	
Install loft hatch and insulate the loft with 250mm thick isowool	
Overboard and skim ceilings to second floor	
PC sum for any repair to roof timbers/leadwork once roof is exposed	£1,500

TIP

Treat writing a schedule of works like writing a shopping list: it is a list of all the works you want to buy.

With a schedule of works in place you will then be able to approach builders to obtain quotes. It is preferable to obtain three competitive quotes so that you can compare the costs. This can be difficult to organise at an auction property; however, it is important to understand, as much as possible, how much the works may cost *before* you buy the property. In my experience, you should be wary of builders who quote day rates or who are vague in their calculations and who claim 'everything will be all right'. This sort of attitude to costing and planning projects normally does not end up 'all right'.

TIP

Be cautious of any quote that is very low and ensure you understand what is and is not included.

Money talks

The British can be quite reserved – and maybe even a little bit embarrassed – when talking about money. But, this is not the time to be shy, embarrassed or 'too backwards in coming forwards'. It is imperative that money is discussed in detail and at length! All costs, now and in the future, must be put on the table for discussion so you can accurately assess the spend required on the project.

It is also important that all quotes and costs are written and agreed so there is no confusion at a later stage of the project. Any and all conditions should be discussed and stipulated in writing from the outset. You must start as you mean to go on: being open, honest and clear in your communication is the only way to ensure a good future working relationship. All costs should be checked, calculated and a contingency sum added. Most developers and investors will allow for an additional 10–15 per cent of the total budget as a contingency sum to cover any unforeseen issues.

Once the costs of the refurbishment works have been calculated, these need to be added to the anticipated price of what the property in its current state is worth. These costs need to be checked against the projected end value of the property to see if there is any margin in the project. If the end value does not add up to more than the anticipated cost of the property plus the renovations then there is little to be gained from any further research. A profit margin must exist to make the project worthwhile. Once this assessment has been made, the next calculation that needs to be added is your time.

Cost what your time is worth

It may sound a ridiculous notion to 'cost your time', as you probably feel you will be more than compensated when the property is sold for a potential big, fat profit. But it is important to realise that you are not working for free – and shouldn't work for free .Many people go into property development thinking they can earn big bucks, but the big bucks are not that easy to come by and it takes a lot of hard graft and risk to achieve. It is therefore important to be realistic and cost your time to ensure you are gaining the best possible results from any project you undertake.

One of the first considerations when costing your time is to work out what you currently earn per day and calculate if you would be better off paying someone else to do the work at the property. If for example, you currently earn £100 per day, and a labourer will cost you £80 per day, it is a simple mathematical sum which shows you would be losing £20 per day working on the project yourself rather than employing a labourer. You may also consider doing the project after work, or at the weekends when you are not at work, so you have the best of both worlds – though this does not always lead to a win-win situation. The project will usually take longer to complete, leading to increased finance costs and could possibly leave you open to changeable market forces.

It is easy to fall into the trap of thinking it is cheaper to do a job yourself than pay somebody else – but this is not always the case. There are two issues at stake:

1. If you do not have the required skill set to undertake the job in hand, it may actually end up costing you more to do the work than if you had employed a professional who knew what they were doing. This is a false economy. Moreover, a skilled professional is more likely to achieve a better finish for the works required

than an amateur. This, again, has an impact on the bottom line and the end value of the project. People are far more willing to pay a premium for a professional finish than an amateur finish.

2. What better uses could you put your time to which could make or save you more money? Again, the use of your time needs to be considered; while you may be happy to give tiling a try, perhaps your time would be better utilised by sourcing quality tiles at a lower price and employing the services of a professional tiler to fit them. The savings made from sourcing cheaper materials then offsets against the cost of the professional tiler.

Be honest and realistic

It is very easy to get carried away and see a renovation project as a chance to learn new skills, save some money by doing it yourself and earn a bit extra on the side – especially if you do it as a sideline to your everyday employment. However, it is important to be honest and realistic with yourself if you want to improve your chances of the project being a success – and for you to make the desired profit. Skills can be learned and the process can be enjoyable, but you need to decide if you are doing a project to learn or to earn. Undertaking a property renovation in order to learn new skills is a very expensive way to educate yourself and there are much cheaper courses available at your local college!

Many people have a romantic vision of the renovation experience – it can be a huge amount of fun – but it is also a colossal amount of hard work and requires a lot of dedication and determination to ensure it gets finished. It is important to be honest with yourself about your current skill set, your commitments and your ability to spend time at the project. At first, your family may not mind the odd weekends and nights spent working on the project, but that goodwill (and your desire to be there all the time) will start to wane. You have to be realistic about whether you can stay the course for the full amount of time the project requires. What may be good for you may not be good for the project, or vice versa!

Calculate the cost of buying at auction

Unless you are buying something which is rare, in high demand or unusual, a property purchased at auction should be bought at a discounted price. There are two key reasons why an auction discount should be built into the calculations of a bid price.

1. **Risk to reward ratio.** Buying property at auction involves a number of risks and the reward for those risks should result in a lower purchase price than if you had bought through an estate agent. In buying property at auction and the speed with which the sale is made, it is critical you price the uncertainties. Following due diligence will enable you to make a confident decision about a property purchase – however, there will often still be unknowns and these must be factored into the bid price. Unless a profitable risk to reward ratio exists there is no commercial incentive to buy at auction rather than through an estate agent.

2. **Time value of money**. The saying: '*Money today is generally worth more than money tomorrow*', is what is known as the *Time Value of Money*. The basic statement is very simple: one pound today is worth more than having one pound tomorrow (or next year). The time value of money is a powerful concept in the auction room – and the simple fact is, when you buy property at auction you expect a discount because you are buying today. The money you have in your pocket today should buy you more than it would tomorrow – that is, buying at auction vs. buying with an estate agent. Discounted deals happen at property auction because of the power of money today.

The level of discount for buying a property at auction will vary depending upon the property itself, the location, the works which are required and the potential opportunity identified. Different buyers look for different discount premiums depending upon the property in question. There are no fixed rules; however, as a general guideline it is usual to expect a minimum of at least a 10 per cent discount for buying property at auction. This discount can fluctuate according to market sentiment and demand for property in a particular area. In sought-after areas, there may be little or no discount.

Selling costs

If you intend to sell a property after refurbishment, this expense also needs to be added into the total costs. There are some people who regularly buy, refurbish and sell property and this is commonly known as 'flipping'. When flipping a property it is critical that the selling costs are added to the total costs as they can amount to quite a hefty sum (as much as 2 per cent of the final value of the property) which could eat into your profits quite heavily. Most people still use high street estate agents to sell their property, but if profits are tight or you want to maximise your reward you could also consider using an online estate agent.

Online estate agents offer the same services as a high street estate agent. The key difference is that you will be required to undertake the property viewings. The online estate agent will list the property for sale with property websites and will liaise with people for viewing appointments which you will conduct. Thereafter any contract negotiation or liaison will continue between the agency and the buyer just as it would with a high street estate agent. This can be a huge cost saving as most online estate agents charge a one-off upfront fee or a far-reduced fee in comparison to a high street estate agent.

How to calculate the bid price of an auction property

The bid price of a property at auction is the culmination of a lot of research, planning, quotes, and valuations. It is at this point when everything comes together to form the bid limit – the final price you are willing to pay for a property at auction. While the journey to arrive at this destination may seem long-winded, laborious and incredibly in-depth, in fact the steps are simple and at each stage will produce a figure that needs to be added to the mix to produce the final amount – the bid price. The easiest way to tally all of the research undertaken is to place a sum next to each of the variables involved. Thus a calculation sheet should involve a simple set of numbers which represent each stage of the process:

1. Market value of property in current state: £...
2. Cost of buying property: £...
3. Cost of works: £...
4. Cost of time: £...
5. Auction discount: £...
6. End value of property when complete: £...

To illustrate this further, a worked example may look like this:

1. Market value of property in current state: £70,000
2. Cost of buying property: £4,000
3. Cost of works: £9,000
4. Cost of time: (30 days @ £100 per day)   £3,000
5. Auction discount: (10 per cent)   £7,000
6. End value of property when complete: £100,000

You will see in the above example that the market value of the property in its current state is £70,000. An auction discount of 10 per cent has been applied. This gives an initial bid price of £63,000. The end value of the property is £100,000. However, to achieve that valuation works are required. Thus the works, buying costs and time involved need to be added to the total figure to ensure a margin exists and that the project will be profitable.

To do this, all costs need to be added to the initial bid price:

1. Initial bid price: £63,000
2. Cost of buying property: £4,000
3. Cost of works: £9,000
4. Cost of time: £3,000
5. Total costs: £79,000

These total costs need to be subtracted from the end value of the property to assess the profitability: £100,000 (end value) - £79,000 (total costs) = £21,000 (profit).

This may seem a reasonable profit for the sum invested. But the best way to understand a project, and to set a bid limit, is by understanding the profit margin.

Profit margin

Calculating the profit margin of a project enables you to compare projects directly against each other and understand the relative performance. Through calculating the profit margin, or the ratio of profit to revenue, you can measure the overall performance, and understand if there is room for manoeuvre when setting a bid limit. In simple terms: the bigger the profit margin = the better the chance of success = the higher the likelihood for an increased bid limit.

To calculate the profit margin the following sum is used:

(profit ÷ price) x 100 = profit margin

Using the previous worked example, this would produce:

(£21,000 [profit] ÷ £100,000 [selling price]) x 100 = 21 per cent [profit margin]

Thus the worked example shows if £63,000 was paid for the property, after all costs and with the end selling price at £100,000 there would be a gross profit margin of 21 per cent. This is a reasonably healthy profit margin, as 15 to 20 per cent is fairly typical of standard property renovations. While it is possible (and advisable) to aim for higher margins, as a general rule, a project should not be undertaken for less than a 10 per cent profit margin. Overspends and overruns are not uncommon and will eat rapidly into the bottom line.

TIP

As a general rule of thumb, a project should not be undertaken for less than a 10 per cent profit margin.

Of course, a 21 per cent profit margin would be great news if this property could be bought at the initial bid price of £63,000 – however, it is important to be realistic and work within a bid limit which gives you the best chance of success. Higher profit margins do still exist, but these are usually priced to reflect the risk of the market and/or the property. Thus, for example, a property without planning, or a property in a less desirable area, will carry higher profit margins to offset against the risk involved: the risk to reward ratio.

If the property under consideration is not of an unusual risk type and you are prepared to accept a lower reward, it is possible to revise the bid limit to reflect a lower profit margin. However, when lowering the profit margin, you must be aware you are increasing the risk of the project as you will have less financial protection as a buffer should renovation costs soar, or the market change causing the final value to decrease.

With this in mind, let us look at how the profit margin of a project can be calculated to produce a bid price which takes the profit margin as the starting point. In the calculation below the profit margin has been set at 15 per cent. The calculation then uses the end selling price minus the total costs (but not including the price of the property) to give you the bid price of the property. To calculate, the following sum needs to be performed:

(1 - 0.15 [profit margin]) x selling price - costs = bid price

Using the previous worked example this would look like this:

(1 - 0.15 [profit margin]) x £100,000 - £16,000 = £69,000

Thus, if the project were to be undertaken at a profit margin of 15 per cent, this would return a profit of £15,000. At this level, it means a bid limit of £69,000 could be paid for the property to produce a profit margin of 15 per cent. In this example, this would mean hardly any discount is being given for purchasing the property at auction. This would require careful consideration before bidding so high. However, if the property is in high demand, rare or unusual an auction discount may not apply.

This worked example and calculations have shown how the initial bid price of £63,000 was arrived at, the potential profit margins involved, and how to assess the margin to create an upper bid limit of £69,000. Thus the bid price for the example property is £63–£69,000, with an anticipated profit margin of 15–21 per cent. If you intend to sell the property once works are complete, the costs of selling need to be factored into your budget.

Evaluating the profit and profit margins of a project are a key way to determine the bid price of a property at auction. In the case of a property which is bought for investment purposes, another form of assessment should also be included in the bid price calculation and this is yield.

How to calculate yields

In the case of a property which is being bought as an investment, the yield needs to be calculated. A yield is made up of two components: the rental yield and the capital yield. In simple terms, a yield is the return expected on the property investment. This is similar to the interest rate received on savings in a bank account. In the case of a property investment, the yield is the property equivalent of the annual interest rate on any savings invested with the bank.

Rental yield

Investment properties which are rented to tenants receive a rental income. To calculate the gross rental yield of a property the annual rental is divided by the purchase price of the property.

(annual rent ÷ price) x 100 = gross rental yield

Thus if a property was purchased for £100,000 and the rental income received per month was £500, the yield calculation would be:

£6,000 (annual rent) ÷ £100,000 (purchase price) x 100 = 6 per cent (gross rental yield)

Simply put, yield is the return on your investment expressed as a percentage of what you put in. These gross yields give an indication of a property's performance. However, a gross yield does not include any property maintenance costs, insurance, mortgage payments, voids, etc. To calculate the net yield of a property it is necessary to include all costs of the property in addition to the purchase price to obtain the net yield figure.

Capital yield

When a property increases in value over time, it is known as **capital growth.** Capital growth, also known as capital appreciation, is the price appreciation on an investment relative to the amount which was initially invested. For example, if a property was bought for £100,000 and the value increases to £150,000, the capital gains yield is 50 per cent. It is calculated as follows:

capital gains yield =
(market price of a property - original purchase price) ÷
original purchase price x 100

Capital gains yields are notoriously difficult to predict and while appreciation has been strong in recent times, the value of the property can go down as well as up. The local market also plays a major role in the capital yield of a property. Factors such as new transport links, regeneration programmes, more affluent buyers attracted to the area and so on can have an impact.

While it is possible to achieve both rental and capital yields, the majority of properties will fall into either one or the other: property which produces higher capital yields vs. property which produces higher rental yields. In general, lower value properties will produce higher rental yields and lower capital yields, whereas higher value properties will produce lower rental yields and higher capital yields. Most investors will normally have a bias to a particular style of property investment, although some may buy a mixture of properties for rental income, while adding to their portfolio with properties envisaged to be stronger in terms of capital growth.

TIP

If your bid limit ends in a 0 or a 5 (for example, £65,000 or £70,000) try to add one more bid to make the limit more uneven, for example, £66,000/£71,000.

If the deal doesn't stack up . . . walk away

It is very easy to get carried away when so much work, time and effort has been put into researching a property prior to auction, but it is essential, if the sums do not stack up, that you walk away. This can be very difficult to do, but buying a property that does not make financial sense is the equivalent of financial suicide. It is important to remain objective. Numbers can be fudged, fiddled and flipped about – but they must be factual – and the facts must be paid attention to. If the property does not make money – and you cannot find a way for it to make money – walk away. One of the best pieces of advice I learnt early on from a very experienced investor is that 'there is always another property'. In the beginning I used to struggle with this because having spent so much time and effort on a property before auction I didn't really want to let it go – but I had to face facts. It is imperative you keep your emotions in check and all facts at the forefront. Property is a hugely emotional purchase and even when buying as an investment it can be difficult to remain detached and objective. However, success relies on the ability to focus on the figures. The figures are what will pay the profit – which is the real success of buying property at auction.

TIP

The numbers do not lie – if a deal does not stack up, walk away.

AUCTIONEER INSIGHT

Regular auction buyers will have four or five properties marked in their catalogue and they don't mind if they buy all of them or none of them. The key factor which will determine the purchase is the price and the limit they have set. Only when the property sells at or below the limit set will they buy. (Guy Charrison, Network Auctions)

Offer to buy before auction

In some cases it is possible and desirable to offer to buy a property before auction. If an offer is accepted before auction, the usual auction sale conditions still apply. This means a 10 per cent deposit will be required and contracts will be exchanged. The sale will complete in the same timeframe as specified in the auction conditions. The only difference with buying a property before auction, is that the property will not be entered for sale in the auction room. This secures the property at a set price rather than the price being dictated by the bidders in the room. The main reason why people offer on a property before auction is to secure the deal. It may be the property has the potential to be very popular in the auction room, thus an offer before auction could secure the property at a competitive price ahead of the sale day and cut out any bidding wars. When offering to buy a property before auction, time is even more important as the deal must be completed ahead of the auction sale date.

The first step in deciding whether an offer should be made on a property before auction should be to assess the likelihood of the vendor accepting the offer. In many cases, the vendor may not be in a situation where it is possible to accept an offer before auction. Properties that are being sold by public bodies (for example, local authorities), or most repossessions will fall into this category. This is because the sale needs to be public and the price achieved proven to be the best price on the day. In these circumstances where an auction sale is required for accountability purposes it is unlikely an offer will be accepted prior to auction. However, this situation can always be confirmed with the auctioneer by asking if the vendor will accept offers prior to auction. In the case of private vendors, this situation will usually depend upon the property, interest levels shown so far, anticipated demand in the auction room and the value of the offer submitted.

Offers made on a property before auction will need to be at an attractive level to entice the vendor to accept and exchange before auction. This means for an offer to be accepted prior to auction it must be at a sufficient level for the vendor to believe a higher price is unlikely to be achieved in the room. A successful offer will usually be in excess of the guide price of the property – although how far in excess will depend upon the property and the demand to secure the sale before auction. This can be a difficult balancing act because, while there is a desire to secure the property before auction, there is also a desire not to pay more than what it may have cost in the auction room. Making an offer before auction is therefore something of a gamble because it is necessary to weigh up the price which may be accepted prior to auction against the price which may be achieved in the auction room. This is a very difficult estimation to make, as you are trying to anticipate and predict other people's behaviour and bidding prices.

The difficulty in trying to predict behaviour and prices at auction is perhaps one of the main reasons why more properties are not sold before auction and, in many cases, the price is left up to the room. What can also happen in the case of offers prior to auction, is the offer received raises the expectations of the vendor's selling price and potentially may increase the price of the property on the day. Thus a property which originally had a reserve of £100,000 may have its reserve increased to £110,000 following an offer before auction. The difficulty with making an offer before auction is that it also shows the auctioneer and the vendor your cards, and leaves very little room for manoeuvre should the offer be rejected. Buying property at auction is akin to playing poker – cards should be kept close to your chest, your face should remain impassive but your mind alert to all potential cards your opponents may hold.

Insider Insight

Calculate what the opportunity is worth to you. Cost the project objectively, but do not be afraid to add in some 'subjective' worth. A property which is located closer to home in a known area may be worth more to you personally than one further away.

Chapter Overview

This chapter has considered the costs of buying a property at auction and the calculations that need to be taken into account when establishing a bid price. Methods for valuing the property have been discussed and research tools have been provided. Any refurbishment works need to be planned, costed and quoted to calculate the margin of a property. It is important to realistically assess your current skill set and available time for a project. Methods for calculating the bid price have been presented and consideration has been given to evaluating the profit, profit margin and rental and capital yield of a property. Property bought at auction requires an understanding of the risk to reward ratio and if a deal stacks up. Offering to buy property before auction can secure the deal and cut out competition in the auction room.

Expert Tip

Money is made when you buy, not when you sell. Buy a property at a good price and you will always make money.

Watch Point

The practice of demanding a contribution towards the vendors' costs of selling at auction is increasing. This can range from reimbursement of legal documents to the costs of the entire sale fees at auction. These costs can add up to thousands and can have a major impact on the profit of a project.

CHAPTER 7

The Big Day has Arrived: Auction Sale Day!

'Going to a property auction was one of the most memorable days of my life . . . it really was such an exciting and nervous time! I still remember the tingles now.'

(Sarah, auction buyer)

Auction sale day is both thrilling and nerve-racking: this is the big day when you will now try to buy the property. Personally, I struggle to sleep the night before an auction sale day – I am so excited about the prospect of bidding for a property at auction. I find myself daydreaming about the bargain price I may be able to buy the property for . . . which then gets interrupted by nightmarish thoughts about my competition in the room and their outbidding me. It really is such an exciting time when all your hopes, dreams and fears come to fruition in one big day. Auction day is the climax of an incredible amount of research, planning and preparation – and the actual sale is over in just a matter of minutes.

Prepare to succeed

It is best to arrive at the auction room at least two hours ahead of the lot you wish to bid for to enable you to check any amendments or announcements relating to the property. It is common practice for last-minute amendments to be added and so it is crucial you are aware of any changes before you bid on a property. The auctioneer will presume any bidder has read and understood the amendments before bidding and these will also form part of the contract of sale.

Most amendments are of an administrative nature, such as correcting auction details or providing further information which was not known at the time of the catalogue publication. However, on some rare occasions an amendment may be made which is of a more consequential and material nature – perhaps the property was vacant and has now been found to be occupied. This may have a major impact on your ability and desire to bid and so will require fast thinking – and maybe even a few phone calls – to decide if you still want to go ahead. Unfortunately, it is also common for properties to be withdrawn from an auction sale or sold prior to auction – even on the actual sale day. This can be very frustrating and disappointing: it is always best to check with the auction house before you leave to ensure the property is still available for sale.

AUCTIONEER INSIGHT

Buyers should arrive at the auction in plenty of time. There are so many occasions where we have had people rush into the room who have got delayed in some way, and who want to know if a lot has been sold. So many people miss lots they want to buy because of not getting to the auction room on time. Invariably it always seems the property was sold for less than what they would have paid and so there is a big sense of disappointment and frustration. (Andrew Binstock, Auction House London)

> ### *TIP*
> Arrive early to check any amendments and survey the room. Calculate the approximate time your bid should be sold and prepare to succeed!

Documents required to bid

Preparation is also required in terms of the documents you will need to have with you to bid and buy at the auction sale. Remember you will need to take documents for all buyers who are to be named on the property purchase, even if they are not in attendance at the auction room. Moreover, if you are buying in the name of a company, you will be required to have a letter signed by the directors giving you authority to bid on behalf of the company. Most auction houses accept cheques for the deposit on a property although some also accept debit card payments, while others may insist on a banker's draft. Cleared funds must be available when bidding as the cheques will be special-cleared, meaning that funds will be requested almost immediately following the auction.

The critical check list you will need with you is:

- One proof of photographic identification (for example, passport, driving licence)

- One proof of residential address dated within the last 3 months (for example, bank statement, utility bill)

- Cleared funds to pay 10 per cent deposit (cheque, banker's draft and/or debit card)

Some auction houses will require you to register before you can bid and so upon arrival at the sale room it is important to check if this is a requirement. If registration is required, you will be asked to produce your forms of identification and they will provide you with a paddle number, this is your identifying number to the auction house when you bid for a property. It is important you keep this paddle number in a safe place as this number will then be connected to your personal details for the property purchase. On some rare occasions, an auction house may require cleared funds before you actually bid – if this is the case, you must ensure the auctioneer has received your monies for you to participate.

LEGAL INSIGHT

If the person who attends an auction is proposing to bid on behalf of themselves and somebody else, then full details of everybody ought to be disclosed to the auctioneers prior to bidding. Normally, the auctioneers will want to see all of the buyers or, at the very least, the person bidding at the auction needs to bring along identification documents for the other buyer/s and show these to the auctioneers. (Michael John Hayward, solicitor).

Keep property details and bid limit to hand

It is advisable to have your property paperwork with you on the day of auction. Having your notes available will allow you to refer back to them should you have any last-minute questions about the property. You should also write down your final bid price on a piece of paper, or on the inside of your wrist, to remind yourself of your final limit. This will enable you to think and act more objectively when the sale starts. Auctions are very exciting and it is easy to get carried away, so it is important to try to remain level-headed and focussed on the task in hand. The bid limit you have set for a property has been set for a reason, therefore it is critical you do not allow yourself to get swept away with auction fever and bid beyond the limit you have set. Buying property at auction is very competitive and can be very emotional; it is essential you keep your emotions in check. Having the bid price written down can help focus your mind and your thinking.

TIP

Write down your upper bid limit to ensure you focus once the auction starts.

Pre-bid nerves – or bigger doubts?

Before the auction begins it is common to suffer from pre-bid nerves. However, if for any reason the emotions you feel are more than pre-bid nerves and are related to the property itself rather than the process of buying it, you should stop, listen and think. Bidding for a property at auction means you may potentially own the property very soon. If you are no longer sure you want to own the property you must think very carefully before bidding. In this situation, it is advisable to leave the auction room, have a short walk or a coffee at a café close by. The reasons for not wanting to buy the property should be written down and if possible discussed with another party. Even if you are on your own at the auction, it is best to call and discuss your reasons with somebody to decide if the change of heart is related to the property or just auction nerves. It can happen that, even after having done all the work and making it to auction sale day, you still feel unsure of the property. In this case, a property should not be purchased. This may sound strange advice given the amount of work and research which has been involved. But the best piece of advice I was taught early on, and which I still believe in and use to this day, is: 'If in doubt, leave it out.' This can seem very difficult to do, especially if you have spent a lot of time and even money before auction, but the simple fact is that if you do buy the property, you will spend an awful lot more time and money when you own it. Be sure before you bid.

TIP

Treat the auction sale day as a day out. Organise to meet friends later and make the most of the day. The actual bidding for the property is over in minutes and afterwards you will definitely want to celebrate or commiserate!

Psychology of the auction room

To look at, the property auction room is just a room. As a venue it does not hold any special significance or meaning. What makes a property auction room special is the whole psychology underpinning the sale and the people in attendance. This psychology is cleverly crafted by the auction house and transforms the room into an auction room which has a unique energy and gives property auctions their magical appeal. The auctioneer plays a key role in creating the sense of drama and excitement on the day – but he also needs a willing audience who will participate in the enjoyment of buying property at auction.

AUCTIONEER INSIGHT

Auction sale day is about creating an environment and an atmosphere where people want to buy. (Andrew Binstock, Auction House London)

The look of an auction sale room

Property auction sales are typically held in large, central venues. Most auction houses will hire a large function room in a hotel, although they are also regularly held in rooms at airports, football stadiums and town halls. For the larger auction houses, the function room will hold approximately 100–150 people seated – although for popular auctions there can be many, many more standing. The layout of the auction room will depend on the auction house and the venue, but usually there will be a main room where the auction sale is located, and an additional room with desks which will have the legal papers in boxes as well as the registration desk. At some property auctions there may also be promotional desks with companies offering auction finance services, property surveys and other related services.

In the main auction room there will be a stage or rostrum at the front where the auctioneer stands. There will also be a large screen located at the front which will display the property being auctioned. Just off the main stage there is usually a desk with a telephone and here sits a member of the auction team who deals with any telephone bids during the auction. Along the side of the auction room, or at the rear, there will be a line of desks with chairs placed at either side. These are known as the contracts desks and this is where contracts are signed should your bid be successful. In the rest of the room and all facing the front, will be multiple rows of chairs for people who want to sit and bid.

The feel of an auction sale room

When you enter an auction sale room, what you see isn't necessarily much – it is what you feel that will make you tingle. The energy bubbles that ripple around an auction room are extraordinary. It is this buzz which hits you as soon as you enter the room. If the auction house has done its job well, the room will be packed – all seats will be taken and the standing room will be a sea of eager faces all keen to participate in the sale. The atmosphere has a jovial edge – everybody wants to bid and buy . . . but not everybody will win. There is a competitive air and this sense of nervous anticipation creates a unique blend of excitement and anxiety which is heightened by the volume of people bustling into the crowded room. The feeling is contagious. It is an energy which seeps into your body and mind – and it is palpable. The feel of a property auction room is like no other – and this is the reason why it is so important to try to keep your head. It may sound strange, but the atmosphere is intoxicating and you can find yourself doing strange things unless you keep a tight rein on yourself.

'Auction fever'

The momentum and energy of an auction room is fast-paced – but also changeable. The mood can turn from hungry excitement to lacklustre boredom in the blink of an eye. It is an energy flow which requires careful and constant management by the auctioneer. Throughout the course of a sale day the momentum of the room will rise and fall according to the lots which are offered and the levels of audience participation. Creating and sustaining interest in the sale is critical to a successful auction. The excitement and competition in the room can fuel bidding wars and the sale price achieved may be far in excess of what anybody had anticipated or predicted. This 'auction fever' is a very real phenomenon and occurs in moments of frenzied bidding where people are overwhelmed by the need to win. It is a battle which is a spectacle to behold with each bidder fully engaged and engrossed in the battle.

In particularly intense bidding wars, a hush will usually descend over the room. It can feel as though everybody has held their breath and is waiting for the next move – for the next bid. Such heated competition will usually culminate in a staggering winning price and a rapturous round of applause from the room. While auction fever doesn't ordinarily reach such gripping and intense levels on a regular basis, it certainly exists at some level throughout the auction sale. It is a sensation which will grab you and urge you on – it will excite you and convince you to raise your hand to make one more bid, even if you have already reached your limit. Auction fever is a pulsating adrenaline buzz which can provoke you into acting 'in the moment', rather like a temporary loss of sanity. It is in these moments when people forget their bid limits and, mesmerised by the auction, end up paying far more for a property than they had planned! This is why it is so important to write down your bid limit and stick to it!

AUCTIONEER TIP

Do not get carried away. Have an upper limit and stick to it.
(Guy Charrison, Network Auctions)

Bid pace and opening prices

Bidding at an auction room is fast-paced with approximately twenty to thirty lots being sold per hour. The auctioneer does not tend to linger over properties. A lot will be offered for sale with the auctioneer proposing an initial price to the room. If no interest is shown, the auctioneer will rapidly reduce the asking price of the lot to try to increase attention. If the room still remains unresponsive he will ask the audience for a starting price – this will usually spark interest and a price will be shouted out from somebody in the room. The auctioneer will then commence bidding from the start price which has been offered by the bidder in the crowd. It is normal for the auctioneer to make an entertaining remark on the absurdity of the price suggested (usually very low) which will further awaken bidders in the room who may not have been paying due attention. This chain of events will usually ignite curiosity within the room and people will start to pay attention to a potential bargain about to be sold.

If the auctioneer is unable to drum up any interest in the lot then he will give fair warning that he will pass the lot over. This means the property will not be offered for sale to the room. This does not happen very often as usually there will be some cheeky audience member who will try their luck with a very low opening bid.

Role of the auctioneer

> *'I am the controller.'*
> (Andrew Binstock, Auction House London)

In the auction room the auctioneer is the main player. He (or very rarely she) is the centre of attention and commands great respect. Like a ringmaster or a conductor, the auctioneer leads the audience. The auction rostrum is his altar and in the auction room the auctioneer is God! A good auctioneer is able to build up a rapport with the room as a whole and also with individual potential bidders. It is an incredibly difficult role to perform because on the one hand the auctioneer must include everybody in the room, but at the same time build a 'one-on-one' relationship with individual bidders – even when they are competing against each other. It is a remarkable feat that the auctioneer can be both friend and foe in the auction room, but a good auctioneer will always make a bidder feel as if he is on their side. It is a unique and very special skill – which is why the auctioneer is the superstar.

AUCTIONEER INSIGHT

The best bit about being an auctioneer is being on the rostrum. You are never happier than when the bids are flying in. It really is the best fun ever! (Guy Charrison, Network Auctions)

Auctioneer tactics

I enjoy having banter with the room. Every auctioneer has their own style, but I like to be friendly and professional. I like to make sure that everybody is feeling relaxed and enjoys the experience. (Guy Charrison, Network Auctions)

Auctioneers have different styles of conducting sales depending upon their personalities and the auction house they represent. However, the key thing to bear in mind is the auctioneer's sole purpose is to get the highest price possible for the property being sold. It can be easy to forget when you are in the thrall of the auctioneer– but he is acting for the client, not you. The auctioneer may make you feel that he's helping you to secure the property, but that is just one of the tactics they use to get you to bid more.

Auctioneers will use a wide range of tactics into getting you to part with your money – from the charm offensive: 'You're bidding so well, I can tell how much you want this'; to the competitive: 'Really, you're going to let him have it now, after you've bid from the start?'; to the regret factor: 'You'll regret not bidding that extra £500 tomorrow, you'll not find another one like this in a hurry.' These remarks are actually sales tactics – they are designed to encourage you to bid again and to stay involved in the sale. The auctioneer is an exceptional reader of people and emotions. He knows what buttons to press to make you act and react – and this is what he will use to engage and entice you to bid. A good auctioneer will be able to play off a number of different bidders against each other, while making them feel individually that they *all* have a chance of winning the property. The auctioneer will use the energy in the room to build the interest and manage the momentum until the crescendo of the final bid.

AUCTIONEER INSIGHT

The auctioneer endeavours to get the best sale price for the seller. He has a duty of care to the seller and the buyer, and to put the gavel down! (Guy Charrison, Network Auctions)

Auctioneer cues: how to watch the auctioneer

It is possible to analyse the auctioneer's behaviour to look for clues about the selling status of a property. Every auctioneer is different and so it is advisable to arrive early and observe his demeanour carefully. With close interrogation there will be some tell-tale clues which will enable you to understand more about the auctioneer's behavioural patterns when selling the properties. This may include small behavioural tics such as lightly lowering the gavel before lifting it high again to indicate a price has not yet met the reserve, or it may be in the phrases he uses such as 'It's in the room to sell', which might indicate a property has met its reserve and the property will be sold to the next bidder. The clues will be extremely subtle; however, if you watch the auctioneer for a period of time you will be able to understand some of the signals. This understanding of the auctioneer's signals prior to bidding on a lot will enhance your response and reactions when it is your turn to bid.

TIP

Many property auctioneers can appear intimidating when standing high on the rostrum – but remember they need you, the buyer – to help them do their job.

Auctioneer code of conduct

The auctioneer reserves the right to bid on behalf of various parties. This is usually included in the conditions of sale and it is a point which will be mentioned in the opening speech. These various parties may include any telephone or proxy bids received, and it does also include the person selling the lot. This right to bid on behalf of the vendor is included in the Sale of Land by Auction Act, 1867. What this means, in practice, is that if an auctioneer is auctioning a lot but the level of bidding has not reached the reserve price, the auctioneer can 'take a bid off the wall' on behalf of the vendor to help move bidding closer to the reserve price.

This bidding pattern can then continue with the auctioneer taking bids off the wall combined with genuine bids from the room until the reserve price is met. On most occasions and, if an auctioneer is good, nobody in the room will question the bidding and it will look and feel like the auction is proceeding as normal.

The reason for this practice is to assist the auctioneer in reaching the vendor's reserve price. It must be remembered that all properties have a reserve price below which the vendor will not sell. Thus the auctioneer's practice of taking a bid off the wall is accepted as a method for the bidding to reach a level which may enable the property to sell.

There are strict rules which govern the practice and auctioneers are not allowed to take a bid off the wall at the reserve price – it must be at least one bid increment below the reserve and cannot be at or above it. Also, when selling on behalf of the vendor, the auctioneer can either bid himself (acting on behalf of the vendor), or take bids from the vendor (or someone who is acting on behalf of the vendor) in the room. It's not the case that the vendor can bring a gang of friends to the auction room and get them all to bid to bump the price up!

TIP

A good auctioneer will be able to create the illusion of bidding – whether or not there are any bids in the room and he will not let on that he is taking bids off the wall.

> ### *AUCTIONEER INSIGHT*
> Property cannot be bought for less than the reserve price and so it is irrelevant if the auctioneer influenced the bidding to enable the reserve level to be met. No buyer should ever feel hard done by if the auctioneer has helped them along. (Andrew Binstock, Auction House London)

How to bid for an auction property

Bidding for a property at auction can seem like a lot of hard work and trying to work out where to stand, how to attract attention, when to bid and how much to bid can all feel very overwhelming. However, bidding at auction is much more an art than a science; so, while it is important to understand the mechanics and psychology of the sale – it really is up to the individual to find out what works best for them.

Have a clear 'eyeball' position

Every bidder has their own personal preference for where they feel more comfortable in the auction room. Some people like to sit at the front, others prefer to hide in a huddle at the side, and then there are those who prefer to stand at the back so that they can get an overview of the entire room. There are no right or wrong places to stand at an auction room; the only rule is that you need to be seen when the time comes to bid. It is important that wherever you locate yourself in the auction room you feel comfortable. It may take some time for your auction lot to come up and so it is best to find a place where you don't mind staying for a while. It is possible to move around the auction room, but it is preferable to pick a spot and stay there so that you can watch, listen and learn as much as possible.

One tip you could use when deciding where to position yourself is to scan the auction room for potential competition. The way you do this is by looking for any familiar faces that you have seen at the property viewing. If you do recognise any people it is advisable to stand away from them, but have them in a clear vision of sight. This means that when the bidding commences you will be able to quickly tell if they are going to be competition or if they are attending for a different lot. It is not unusual for people to attend auction with the intention to buy two or three lots, depending on the bid levels of the sale.

Before your lot is offered to the room it is essential to know that you can be seen clearly by the auctioneer. The best way to test this is to ensure you can see the actual eyeballs of the auctioneer. You must be able to quickly make direct eye contact with the auctioneer should you wish to bid. If you cannot see the auctioneer's eyeballs, you should position yourself so that you can. Ideally this should be done on the preceding lot to the one you are interested in. This means when your lot is offered for sale you are ready to go.

AUCTIONEER TIP

If you stand at the back you will be able to see the competition and survey the room. You will then be able to pick up when the frantic bidding is happening and when you need to come in. (Andrew Binstock, Auction House London)

Attracting the auctioneer's attention and bidding styles

How you attract the auctioneer's attention and your bidding style is a personal choice. There are no formal rules about what you can and can't do. The most important thing is that should you wish to place a bid, the auctioneer quickly understands that is your intention. The auctioneer is the 'main man' at the auction house and when the bidding has started he will be hawkishly scanning the room looking for interested parties. In addition to the auctioneer there will also be auction spotters from the auction house dotted around the room and on the main stage. These spotters are also on the lookout for any potential bidders whom the auctioneer may have missed and will signal to the auctioneer the location of any people who are interested in bidding. It is important to note that nobody else except the auctioneer can accept a bid on a property. Even if the person is an employee of the auction house, it is the auctioneer with whom you must always place your bid.

Gaining attention to place a bid can be done in a number of ways. You will see that some people have very small body gestures which they use to indicate a bid, such as a nod of their head or a small tap of a finger against their leg. Other people may have much more expansive gestures such as holding up a catalogue or raising their arm. Some people, myself included, have also even been known to shout in an auction room! This is not commonplace and I would not advise it as a regular way to bid. But if needs must and you have to attract the auctioneer's attention, it is better to shout and be heard than be too quiet and be ignored. It is also important to note that the auctioneer's decision is final. If he did not see you bid, then you did not bid. You must always make sure your bid has been acknowledged and accepted by the auctioneer. If in any doubt, you should point to yourself and mouth 'me?', or if needs be, say it out loud to be completely sure.

CASE STUDY: SOMETIMES A GIRL HAS TO DO WHAT A GIRL HAS TO DO!

I was once at a packed auction house. It was being held in a big hotel in Central London. The auction room was the hotel's ballroom and it was very glitzy and glamorous. The auction had attracted a huge number of buyers and it was very difficult to find anywhere to stand. I had just managed to find a small spot where I could see the auctioneer and I was ready to bid. Just as my lot came onto the screen and the bidding had started, two very tall men came and stood right in front of me. I was about to say 'Excuse me!' when I realised they were bidding on my lot. I was so frustrated and angry. I quickly pushed past them and tried to get myself to a different location in the room, all the while keeping my eye on the auctioneer and listening to the frantic pace of the bidding.

It was very difficult to move as the room was crammed and I kept stepping on people's toes and having to jump up and down to try to see what was happening. My heart was absolutely pumping and I was so distressed that I wouldn't be able to bid. Suddenly, I heard the bidding had slowed and then come to a stop, I could hardly see anything for all the shoulders and heads about me. The auctioneer started his final patter: 'Going once . . . going twice . . .'

Desperate not to lose out, I pushed myself through a throng of people and waved my hands manically at the auctioneer – who I still couldn't see at this point. In a frantic state I just shouted at the top of my lungs while struggling with people's limbs, 'Here! here! I want to bid.' The whole room fell silent. I was so distracted by my struggle to bid I didn't even feel embarrassed – I was just desperate to be heard. I don't know if it took everybody by surprise but the auctioneer heard my shouts and the hammer came down on my bid – the final bid! I remember whooping with joy and the auctioneer exclaimed 'Another happy customer!' at which everybody laughed like a sitcom audience.

When to bid?

> 'Most regular auction goers will sit for the first two rounds of bidding and will wait for the auctioneer to struggle. However, in the end the property will sell at its rightful price.'
>
> (Andrew Binstock, Auction House London)

- Similarly to *how* you want to bid, *when* you want to bid is also a matter of personal choice. There are no right or wrong ways – although there are two conflicting schools of thought on when you should bid.

- **Bid early.** The thinking behind bidding early is that the auctioneer knows you are interested in the lot from the outset. This means he will always refer back and include you in the bidding process, unless you signal you are no longer interested. The early interest also signifies to other potential buyers in the room you are competition – you are here to bid and buy and are getting on with it! Bidding early shows intent to buy a lot, and thus may also prevent any additional competition from entering the fray. Bidding early may also have the effect of increasing the price beyond a level which another bidder would be willing to pay – which could mean you buy the lot at a more competitive price.

- **Bid late.** The philosophy of bidding late is to jump in at the last minute and snatch the lot by taking the auction room by surprise. How late to bid is a controversial question – some people will wait until the hammer has almost fallen. This happens in the final seconds of the auction when a bidder may have thought they were about to win the lot. This element of surprise so late in the sale is believed, by some, to knock the other person off balance. This can work as a bidding tactic, though it is quite a well-known trick to seasoned auction goers. The major risk involved is that you might bid too late and the auctioneer will not accept the bid and hence, you lose the sale.

CASE STUDY: DON'T FAN THE FLAMES

Personally, I tend to bid late – but not *too late* for fear of not getting my bid in. Early on in my property auction buying career I sat next to a seasoned auction professional. I watched him buy multiple properties and every time after he had completed the contracts he returned to sit next to me. When my lot appeared and it was soon going to be time to bid, I felt very nervous about sitting next to such an auction expert. The auctioneer had started the bidding for my lot and the bidding appeared to slow down and so I started to raise my arm to bid. The auction professional next to me pulled my arm back and said: 'No, not yet. Wait.'

I was taken aback, but at the same time I decided to trust him. He looked at me and whispered: 'I will tell you when.' I don't know whatever possessed me to trust this stranger, but I did. Within a few minutes the bid price of the lot had escalated and then lulled again. Bidding had almost stopped and the auctioneer had started his final selling call: 'Going once . . . going twice.' I sat staring at the auctioneer and nervously glancing at the stranger next to me who was still holding my arm in a vice-like grip. All of a sudden the auction professional raised my arm. The auctioneer saw me and accepted my bid. I was quite sure I detected a slight sigh on the auctioneer's lips. The other party bid again, so I bid again. Then my competitor shook his head. The property was about to be knocked down to me. I bought it. Elated by my win, but perturbed by the stranger's actions, I questioned him: 'Why did you stop me bidding earlier?' He replied sagely: 'Don't fan the flames; don't pour petrol on the fire, let them have their party and then at the end you will be the one with the can of water to put the fire out.' To this day, it is a philosophy I have always cherished and followed and I am thankful to have had this strange experience.

How much to bid?

The level of the auctioneer's bid increments will vary according to the reserve price of the property and the stage of the bidding process. The auctioneer has a reserve price he needs to meet and so it is important for him to feel the price can be achieved from the bid level proposed. There is one auctioneer whose favourite saying when the bidding starts is: 'It doesn't matter where you start, it's where you end up that's important.' This is very true; however, auctioneers prefer to be able to regulate the bid increments themselves rather than audience members suggesting alternative amounts – but that is not to say you can't ask.

Most bidding in the beginning will start with larger bid increments as the auctioneer is keen to move the room to a price which is within reach of the reserve. However if the bidding slows, the amounts can be varied to try to garner further interest or additional bids. It is common practice for a lot to start with much larger bid increments and for those to reduce to much smaller amounts as the bidding nears the end. The auctioneer will often use the tactic of reducing bid increments to try to squeeze every last penny (or rather pound) from the bidders in an attempt to extract a higher final sale price.

Whilst the auctioneer prefers to regulate the bid increments, it is possible to offer a different increment than the auctioneer proposes. This bid increment can be both higher and lower:

- **Higher bid increment.** This is also known as a 'jump' bid. This can be used by people to upset the rhythm of the bidding and jump the bidding to the next price level. As an example: a lot is being bid for in £1,000 increments, the auctioneer asks for the next bid at £163,000, but a jump bid is proposed by a bidder to £170,000. The auctioneer will usually be delighted at such a higher bid and will accept this. The tactic behind a jump bid is to declare to the room the serious intent to purchase the lot and is in a way a scare tactic which is meant to convince any opponents you will outbid them – and so they should give up now! A jump bid also interrupts the rhythm of the auction and could potentially put competitors off their game when introduced. Jump bids are mainly used by seasoned auction professionals.

AUCTIONEER TIP

A 'jump' bid can blow people out; it is confident and can work to your advantage. It says to the room: 'Look, I am here to buy this.' (Guy Charrison, Network Auctions)

- **Lower bid increment.** Reducing the size of the bid amount can work in two ways. Firstly, it may be used by people who have reached, or are close to their limit, and thus the bid amount is reduced to reflect this. Secondly, it can be used as a 'distraction ploy' to make other bidders think they have bid more than they actually have. Thus, if the bid increments were £5,000 and are reduced to £1,000, the opposing bidder will have to bid five times more to reach the same bid level as before. This tactic can lead some bidders to thinking they have bid more and withdraw from the sale.

It sounds incredulous that such simple tricks can work. However, it must be remembered that these decisions are made under tremendous pressure when in the heat of the auction room. The psychology of the auction room and the tactical methods that can be used to create success should never be underestimated.

TIP

Never be afraid to request a different bid increment – the worst thing that can happen is that the auctioneer will say no.

> ### *AUCTIONEER INSIGHT*
>
> You can never know somebody else's psyche, but I have seen jump bids work more often than not in the auction room. Jump bids disrupt the flow of the room and the rhythm of the bidding. If bidding was in £1,000 increments and you jump the bid by £5,000, the auctioneer will look to the under-bidder for a similar-sized bid increment. This disrupts the expectations of the other bidders and as a tactic can blow people out. (Guy Charrison, Network Auctions)

CASE STUDY: CHANGING THE BID AMOUNT CAN WORK IN YOUR FAVOUR

I had seen a building going to auction which I wanted to bid on, but unfortunately was unable to attend the actual sale day. I much prefer being in the room to bid, and so I asked Alan, a member of staff, to attend on my behalf while I was on the other end of the phone. When the bidding started I requested Alan to act as my eyes and ears in the auction room and repeat every word the auctioneer said and tell me every bid that was made. I sat at the other end of the phone listening intently.

The bidding started extraordinarily slowly and at one point I almost lost my nerve when the auctioneer could not gain any opening interest and declared to the room: 'Well, if nobody is interested in buying this lot we may as well move on . . .' I was panting at the other end of the phone and asking Alan to look all around him to see if anybody was going to start bidding. After what felt like an age, the bidding finally commenced. It was very laborious and every bid seemed to be dragged out of the audience. Bidding then seemed to halt completely and it appeared the property was about to be knocked down. I was poised and ready to bid.

All of a sudden and out of nowhere, a bidding frenzy seemed to overtake the room and the price suddenly doubled in a matter of minutes. I sat transfixed at the other end of the phone. The bidding was almost at my limit and I hadn't even got to bid! Then another competitor entered the fray and my bid limit was reached. I was so disappointed; it had seemed from the outset that I would be buying the building for less than my limit – now that had been reached and I was out of the game. I shrieked down the phone to Alan: 'Is anybody else bidding, what can you see?' Alan looked all around him to try to see if anybody else was going to bid. The price was at my limit, but I didn't want to leave it. The auctioneer had been taking £1,000 bids, but I couldn't stretch to that. Suddenly I found myself bellowing down the phone to Alan: 'Tell the auctioneer £250.'

I could hear Alan in the auction room shouting out my orders: '£250.'

Even though I was not in the room I could imagine the auctioneer's eyes turn and swivel disdainfully.

The auctioneer retorted quizzically: '£250?'

'£250,' Alan repeated.

There was silence while the auctioneer considered the bid amount.

'OK, £250,' the auctioneer responded (in a most resigned tone of voice).

The room continued its silence from this interjection. No more bids were taken. No more bids were offered. The auctioneer knocked down the property to Alan (and me at the end of the phone) for just £250 more than my bid limit!

Alternative methods to bid

Most people who intend to buy property at auction still

prefer to attend the auction room in person to bid. This is because in the room you are able to get a full sense of the action of the auction and are also able to pinpoint potential competitors. However, if for any reason you are unable to attend the auction on the day, there are several alternative ways to bid for a property at auction.

Telephone bidding

Telephone bidding is a popular way to bid for a lot if you are unable to attend the property auction. This needs to be organised and approved with the auction house in advance of the sale day. It is advisable to allow sufficient time (preferably two working days) before the auction sale date to confirm with the auction house they have received your bidding instructions. The auction house will have a telephone bidding form which you will be required to complete and return to them. You will also be required to send proof of your ID and address (in the same way that you would if you were in the auction room). The deposit funds (10 per cent of the final bid price) and the buyer's premium will also need to be supplied to the auction house in advance of the sale. How these funds are to be received will vary, so it is advisable to check with the auction house before submitting a bidding form.

Although telephone bidding is a convenient alternative way to bid, there are drawbacks as the auction house will know your maximum bid price in advance of the sale. Some buyers feel uncomfortable with this as they think this information may lead to the reserve price being increased or it may influence the auctioneer's starting price for the lot. A further disadvantage is that your bid limit form and deposit cheque would have been sent a few days prior to the auction. This may be an issue if you decide you want to bid more because it will be up to the auctioneer's discretion whether to accept a higher bid from you. Lastly, a telephone bid is reliant on the auction house being able to contact you at the time of the auction sale. If they cannot contact you by phone, your bid will not be submitted.

CASE STUDY: THE CASE OF THE MISSED TELEPHONE BID

Several years ago I organised a telephone bid on a property I was interested in. I contacted the auctioneers and submitted the necessary forms, documents and funds to them. On the day of the auction sale the auction house contacted me first thing in the morning to check the telephone number was correct and the line was working. It was anticipated the lot I intended to bid on would be between 2.00 and 3.00 p.m. At 3.00 p.m. my phone still had not rung. I wanted to contact the auction house, but was concerned that if I called them, I would then tie up the phone line they would be trying to call me on. By 4.00 p.m. I realised it was now far too late for the lot and so I contacted the auction house at the room.

I soon learned I had missed the lot by almost two hours and the property had been sold at a knockdown price. I was not very happy and I confronted the auction house staff about why I had not been contacted to bid by telephone. I was informed that they had tried and failed to establish contact and so my bid was not placed. I have no idea what happened as my telephone was working and ready – I just never got that call to bid. However, to this day, this experience makes me nervous about organising telephone bids and wherever possible I always try to attend, or request somebody else attend on my behalf.

NetworkAuctions

AUTHORISATION FORM FOR BIDDING BY TELEPHONE OR PROXY

Name .... ◯ **Telephone** (tick)   ◯ **Proxy** (tick)

Address ....

TELEPHONE NUMBERS

Business ....   **Home** ....   **Mobile** ....

Email ....

I hereby authorise Network Auctions Limited ("the Auctioneers") to bid on my behalf whether by proxy or by telephone for the property referred to below subject to the Terms and Conditions for Bidding by Telephone or by Proxy published in the Auctioneers' catalogue and subject also to the General Conditions of Sale and the Special Conditions of Sale applicable and to any addendum produced at or prior to the Auction.

Address of Lot ....

Lot No. ....

Maximum bid (Figures) ....   (Words) ....

N.B. The bid must be a specified amount. A bid which is expressed to be relative to any other bid will not be accepted. I attach a bankers draft for 10% of the maximum bid. If my bid is successful I confirm the Auctioneers are authorised to sign the Memorandum of Agreement on my behalf.

Solicitors ....   **Solicitors Tel No.** ....

Contact Name ....

Solicitors Address ....

Signed ....   **Date** ....

TERMS & CONDITIONS FOR BIDDING BY TELEPHONE OR PROXY

1. A prospective buyer wishing to make a telephone bid (a "Bidder") must complete, sign and date the form within this catalogue. Separate forms must be completed for each lot on which a bid is to be placed.

2. The form must be delivered to Network Auctions Limited, 133 The Parade, Watford, Hertfordshire. WD17 1NA at least 24 hours prior to the start of the Auction together with the appropriate payment as mentioned below.

3. Forms must be accompanied by a deposit payment of 10% of the Bidder's maximum bid. The deposit payment shall be made by bankers draft. Cheques can only be accepted if provided to the Auctioneers in sufficient time for them to clear through the banking system prior to the Auction.

4. In the case of a proxy bid the Bidder hereby authorizes the Auctioneers or their staff to bid on their behalf as their agent up to the maximum amount of the authorised bid the whole of the Bidder's deposit will be used as deposit towards the purchase price. If the

Bidder is unsuccessful the full amount of the Bidder's deposit will be refunded to the Bidder promptly after the Auction (without interest).

5. In the case of a telephone bid a member of the Auctioneers' staff will attempt to contact the Bidder by telephone before the lot in question is offered for sale. If contact is made the Bidder may compete in the bidding through the Auctioneers' staff. However if telephone contact cannot be made or the connection is lost the Bidder hereby authorises the Auctioneers and their staff to bid on their behalf up to the maximum authorised bid for the lot in question. If the Bidder is successful at a price which is less than the guide price the whole of the Bidder's deposit will be used as a deposit towards the purchase price. If the Bidder is unsuccessful the full amount of the Bidder's deposit will be refunded to the Bidder promptly after the Auction (without interest).

6. If the Bidder is successful the Bidder hereby authorises the Auctioneers to sign the Memorandum of Agreement on their behalf.

7. If the Bidder wishes to withdraw or alter his instructions or to attend the Auction to bid it is their responsibility to notify the Auctioneers in writing before the Auction and also to notify the auctioneer in charge of the Auction before the lot in question is offered for sale.

8. The Auctioneers shall not be liable for any failure to bid due to inadequate or unclear instructions being received or for any other reason. The Auctioneers have absolute discretion as to whether or not and in what manner to bid.

9. The Bidder is deemed to have full knowledge of the General and Special Conditions of Sale and the Notice to All Prospective Buyers herein. The Bidder is also deemed to have full knowledge of any addendum produced by the Auctioneers at or prior to the Auction. The Bidder is therefore advised to check whether any relevant addendum has or will be produced but the Auctioneers will not be liable to the Bidder if he fails to so check.

(Source: Network Auctions, 2013)

Proxy bidding

A proxy bid is where you instruct the auctioneer to bid on your behalf at the auction. This requires similar administration as a telephone bid (ID documents, 10 per cent deposit and buyer's premium) and will involve completing a proxy bid form. This works in a similar way to the telephone bid and will require you to plan your maximum bid in advance. The key difference with a proxy bid is that no further communication with you is required – the auction house will bid on your behalf in the room. This has the same disadvantages as the telephone as it means the auction house knows in advance the maximum bid from an interested party. The key advantage over the telephone bid is the instruction is there for the auctioneer to bid on your behalf. In my personal case study above, if I had used a proxy bid rather than a telephone bid, I believe I would have bought the property rather than missing it because communication could not be established.

By someone else

If you are unable to make it to the auction, it is possible for somebody to attend and bid on your behalf. This could be a professional (for example, a solicitor or surveyor) or it could be a close friend or family relative. It is important to make sure that the person attending on your behalf is trustworthy and able to cope with the stress of the auction. You should also ensure they have all the documents required and cleared funds to be able to bid.

Online

Surprisingly, no mainstream auction houses currently use the technology available to allow for bidding online. However,

I am sure in the future online bidding will become increasingly commonplace. Similarly to the above distant-bidding methods, I would envisage that registration would be required ahead of the sale date. However, unlike current distant-bidding methods, online bidding would allow bidders much more flexibility and control.

TIP

It is always best to bid at the auction room, so, where possible, try to attend the sale day.

AUCTIONEER INSIGHT

Proxy bids and telephone bids are alternative ways to bid if you are unable to attend on the day. These bids are designed to work on the same basis as if you were in the room and should not disadvantage buyers. As the auctioneer, I do not have the bid limit disclosed to me and the staff act as though they are actually a bidder in the room, on the buyer's behalf. (Guy Charrison, Network Auctions)

Do a dummy auction run

Buying a property at auction is an exhilarating roller coaster ride culminating in the final auction sale day when you hope that all of the research and preparation you have done will come to fruition. Auction sale day on its own is a terrifyingly exciting experience and the energy and buzz of the room can really sweep you off your feet. It is advisable therefore to try to experience a property auction as a dry run ahead of attending and bidding on a property for real.

Test experience: practise buying a property at auction

Attending an auction when you do not intend to buy, may seem a little meaningless unless you actually have a property of interest and which you know something about. As an onlooker you will be able to experience some of the energy and excitement of the auction atmosphere, but to really understand if you are on the right track you need to have a proper test experience. What this means is to practise buying a property, follow it through to the auction – but don't actually bid. Practising buying a property at auction is rather like a virtual property auction game – you get to experience all the real research and properties available – but you don't actually spend a penny. It is recommended you treat the practice auction property as if it was a real property – just with some minor tweaks to the research to avoid any unnecessary costs. The knowledge, insights and analysis gained will equip you with the skills you need to successfully buy property at auction.

Practise research – but do it in real life!

- Identify an auction property of interest.

- Check the legal paperwork – does the property sound good on paper?

- View the property.
  - Be a surveyor.
  - Turn detective.

- Check the legals as if you were a solicitor.
  - Ask the vendor's solicitor some of the questions that you envisage your solicitor may have asked.

- Find out how to finance the property – ask questions of your bank, mortgage broker and find out what requirements are needed for them to be able to lend.

- Research the property market.
  - Check the online resources and estimate a value for the property.
  - Speak to estate agents to check your valuation figures.

- Obtain quotes for the works planned.
  - Request builders to attend and quote on the works you plan to do.
- Calculate the bid price you are prepared to pay.
  - Set your bid range.

- Attend the auction and watch the practice property sell in the room.
  - Observe the action in the room – was it a popular or unpopular lot?
  - How close was your bid limit to the final selling price?
    ◊ What could you do differently to ensure you will be the winning bidder next time?

Practice research on real properties will boost your understanding of the market and enable you to bid successfully at auction in the future.

Unsold property

Overall sales statistics for auction rooms show that on average 75 per cent of property entered for auction is sold at auction. In fact there are some extremely successful auction houses which can boast a sale rate of over 90 per cent. This means if a property is entered for sale at auction it is more than likely to sell. However, there are some occasions when a property does not sell. The main reason why properties do not sell at auction is because they failed to meet the reserve price set.

If a property fails to meet its reserve it will be classified as unsold, however it will still be available for sale after the auction, usually at the reserve price. The main advantage of buying unsold property after auction is that the auctioneer will generally disclose the reserve price. This removes a lot of the guesswork which is involved when planning to bid at auction. Many buyers will buy unsold properties after auction and this practice, which is known in the business as 'hawking', is fairly common.

Buying after auction is no less stressful than buying in the auction room – time is critical and auction conditions still apply. If you decide to buy after auction, you will need to exchange contracts and pay the 10 per cent deposit and buyer's premium immediately. There is no difference with the process – it just means that the hammer did not fall on the bid. What is important to note, is that should another buyer also be interested in the property after auction, it is the first person to submit the monies and exchange contracts who wins.

TIP

Buying unsold property at auction is a race to exchange – the first to exchange wins.

CASE STUDY: RESERVE PRICE NOT MET . . . AND THEN EXCEEDED

A five-bedroom property in central Brighton was entered for sale in a London auction house. It had a guide price of £220,000-plus. The property was detailed as tenanted and internal viewings would not be possible. Initial research suggested that the property could be worth as much as £300,000. On a sunny day I decided I should take a day trip to Brighton to view the property. I went along armed with the property information; I had the rental agreement with me and so I knew the names of the tenants and the amount of rent they should be paying. From the outside the property looked to be in a tired condition and some slipped tiles on the roof suggested there might be some potential internal damage. The property looked large from the front elevation, but very narrow from the side: this made it difficult to envisage how five bedrooms would be arranged in the property.

After standing outside and staring at the property for some time, I decided I would try my luck and knock on the door to see if any of the tenants were available to show me around. As luck would have it one of the tenants answered the door. She was initially highly suspicious of this stranger who wanted to look around her home and it was only when I showed her the copies of her tenancy agreement that she agreed I was a genuine interested buyer and was happy to show me around.

The property was in a dated condition and required substantial repair. While listed as having five bedrooms, the property was actually a four-bedroom house, with the fifth bedroom being the lounge (but which was arranged as a bedroom). The tenant helpfully showed me around and told me a lot of the history of the property and the problems they'd had. Having viewed the property internally I decided against bidding on it due to the level of work required and the size of the property being smaller than I had originally anticipated.

The Brighton property was offered to the room but it failed to meet its reserve. I was not surprised by this as I felt perhaps the price had been a little top heavy once I had viewed inside. However, I wanted to know if a deal could be struck and so I called the auction house to discuss the reserve price, which was disclosed to me as being £220,000. I informed the auction house that I would think about it and return to them in an hour. Just 40 minutes later the telephone rang – it was the auction house. They had received a flurry of after-sale auction offers and the property was now going to best and final offers. 'What about the reserve price?' I asked. They replied: 'You will need to pay more than the reserve price now if you want to buy it.' I decided against getting involved in a bidding war after auction. Later that same day the property sold for £240,000. Just imagine: if that buyer had been in the auction room just a few hours earlier he could have bought it for £20,000 less!

Property withdrawn

Unfortunately, property entered for auction is sometimes withdrawn, and this can also happen at quite a late stage – even up until the day of auction. It is advisable to call the auction house the day before the sale to check the property will still be sold at auction. If a lot you were interested in has been withdrawn, the vendors have no responsibility to you for any abortive costs you may have incurred. This can feel most frustrating – especially when you have spent time and money on researching an auction lot. Vendors withdraw properties from auction for a number of reasons, but the main ones are:

- **Sold prior to auction.** This sale could be as a result of being entered into auction, or it could be that a sale was agreed as a private treaty with an estate agent beforehand. As previously discussed, a number of properties are offered for sale with estate agents before they end up in the auction room. It is important to remember properties which are entered for auction are there to be sold. This means vendors are usually very motivated to sell – hence an acceptable offer before auction may work in the favour of some vendors.

- **Incomplete/missing legals.** The tight timescale of property sold at auction requires a quick turnaround of the legal documentation. Any delays with the management company, freeholder, council and so forth can create major issues for the solicitor and auction house. It may be decided on some occasions, if the legal paperwork is so delayed or incomplete, to withdraw the property from auction and enter it at a future date when the paperwork is complete.

- **Incorrect details.** Great care is taken in preparing an auction catalogue; however, due to time constraints, sometimes information which is delayed does not get entered or provided until a very late stage. On occasion this can mean the auction house may make the decision to withdraw the lot from the sale until full details can be confirmed. Alternatively, it may be that the vendor's solicitor does not have sufficient time to ensure the property contract is ready for sale and they advise the property should be withdrawn from sale.

- **Change of mind.** In some cases a property is withdrawn from auction simply because the vendors change their mind. This is not a common occurrence due to the costs involved in entering a property for auction. Unlike selling a property with an estate agent, there can be considerable costs the vendor will have to pay upfront to the auctioneer for the marketing of the property. These upfront marketing fees (which cover the cost of the brochure and viewings, etc.) can amount to hundreds if not thousands of pounds. This fee will be lost if the vendor withdraws from the auction sale and thus it is not a decision that is taken lightly.

If a property you are interested in does get withdrawn from auction, it is advisable to contact the auctioneer to ascertain the reasons and find out if the property may be entered again in a future auction. It may just be a case of delayed paperwork and the property will be available at the next auction – so it's always worth checking.

CASE STUDY: THE CONTINUALLY WITHDRAWN FLAT

I viewed a flat in South London which I fell in love with. It was only small but was well located and next to a park. I did all my homework on the property (as much as I could as the main legals were not available) and waited. I called the auction house almost every day to chase the paperwork. Finally, the day before the auction, they withdrew the property due to missing paperwork. I was assured the paperwork would be sorted and the property should be in the next auction. So I waited. The next auction came around and the property was not in it. Nor was it in the following auction.

Six months went by and I forgot about the flat that I had hoped to bid on. Then suddenly there it was again in the auction catalogue! I was very excited and all ready. I then waited for the rest of the legals. I chased continuously. How could this be happening again? The property was withdrawn just four days after the catalogue publication – the same paperwork was missing. Another four months passed. Then the flat appeared again. I attended the viewing again to make sure the flat was still something I wanted to buy. It was smaller than I remembered, but I still liked the look of it and wanted to bid. I patiently waited for the legals, which at long last were finally released, and did not show any major problems. I organised my bid limit and prepared myself for auction. It had been a very long wait to bid for the property and I was very excited, but on the day of auction I was royally outbid. So perhaps it's not always true that good things come to those who wait.

Insider Insight

It is very easy to get caught up in the excitement of auction and so it is important to keep a clear head and your guard up. Some auction houses offer free wine and nibbles to attendees to relax the mood at auction – this usually leads to higher than average prices being paid.

Chapter Overview

This chapter has looked at what happens on auction sale day and what to expect. Attending the room early is advisable to check any last-minute amendments and to ensure you are there on time to bid. The auction room has a special energy which is contagious and auction fever is a very real phenomenon. Buying at auction is fast-paced and many decisions are made under pressure. Because of this, simple tricks can be used to improve bidding success. In the auction room the auctioneer is God and his decision is final. Auctioneers will use many tactics to increase bidding and will sometimes bid 'off the wall' to ensure a successful sale. How and when to bid is a personal style, and bidding should be regarded as an art form rather than a science. A practice run of buying a property at auction is recommended to prepare for the real thing. Properties that did not sell at auction, and the reasons why, have been discussed, along with the opportunity to buy property after auction.

Expert Tip

Never be afraid to change your mind before bidding. If a property does not feel right, do not feel pressurised to buy.

Watch Point

Last-minute changes to auction particulars can have a serious impact on the value of the property you are planning to bid on. Any amendments should be checked thoroughly before bidding.

CHAPTER 8

After Auction: What Next?

'I didn't really believe it had been me who was bidding when the hammer came down . . . but then someone from the auction house was by my side, and I realised I had just bought a house!'

(Jenny, auction buyer)

After all the research, planning, preparation and excitement of bidding at auction, the hammer actually falling on your bid can sometimes feel unreal. The heady mix of adrenaline and fear coupled with the relief and joy can make the whole experience feel quite surreal. The moments of auction pass in a blur – but the bureaucracy following the auction action is necessary to ensure you have a correct record of events.

Exchange of contracts

In auction law, the moment of contract is the point at which the auctioneer bangs down his gavel. The memorandum that takes place afterwards is simply documenting the existence of the contract. Importantly, the auctioneer has the legal right to sign the contract on behalf of the vendor and also on behalf of the buyer. This is a convenient arrangement which means the vendor of the property does not have to be present at the auction, or if the buyer has bid by telephone or proxy.

Once the gavel has fallen, there is no opportunity to default on a bid. Even leaving the auction room does not get

MEMORANDUM

I/we...

of...

Home Tel. .... Mobile/Business Tel. ....

Email ....

Do hereby confirm that I have this day purchased the property described in the aforementioned Particulars of Sale

as Lot Number ....

Address ....

....

in the sum of £................................... Subject to the General/Common and Special Conditions and that I have

paid to NETWORK AUCTIONS LTD, The Auctioneers, the sum of £................................... as a deposit and in part

payment of the purchase price and I hereby agree to pay the remainder of the said purchase money and to complete the said

purchase according to the aforementioned Particulars and the General/Common and Special Conditions of Sale.

Dated.. day of 2012

Purchase Money.. Administration Fee £495 + VAT

Sub Total.. Less Deposit.............................

Balance to Pay..

Buyers Signature..

As Agents for the Seller ....

we hereby confirm this sale and acknowledge receipt of the deposit in accordance with the within Conditions.

Signed on behalf of the Seller ....

Abstract of Title to be sent to...

....

Tel No. .... Contact Name. ....

(Source: Network Auctions, 2013)

you off the hook, as the auctioneer can sign on your behalf. It is very rare for people to bid and then attempt to leave an auction room without completing the contracts; but it is worth noting there is always a high number of auction staff in attendance to ensure contract paperwork is completed. It is also a common feature of auction rooms to have video cameras – although this seems to be used more for future marketing purposes than to identify auction absconders.

Once you have made a successful bid and the gavel has fallen, a member of the auction house will locate you as the successful bidder and accompany you to the contracts desk. At the desk you will sign a Memorandum of Contract. The Memorandum is a brief contract which includes the following details:

- The auction lot number and address details of property.

- The final hammer price of the property and deposit payable.

- The name of the buyer/s.

- The amount of the buyer's premium.

The Memorandum will usually be attached to the auction catalogue details to ensure the lot number and property details are linked to the contract. On the Memorandum there will be a sum area which details the purchase price, deposit paid and the balance to be paid on completion. One copy will be signed and dated by the buyer and the other copy will be signed and dated on behalf of the vendor. The two documents are then exchanged. It is at this stage where you will need to provide your forms of identification, your 10 per

cent deposit (or the minimum amount specified by the auctioneer), pay the buyer's premium and supply your solicitor's
details. If a solicitor has yet to be instructed – now is the time
to do so. It is important to bear in mind that cheques will be
special cleared and so you must make sure you have funds
available to cover the deposit. A bounced cheque at auction
may not only attract civil proceedings from the vendor but
also criminal proceedings.

LEGAL TIP

Buyers should always give full and proper particulars of all the
people who intend to purchase the property to the auctioneers
and make sure that the names of all the buyers are entered
onto the sale and purchase contract. The seller's solicitors can
refuse to add extra names onto the transfer documentation at
a later stage because the buyer failed to mention those other
persons to the auctioneers at the time the contract was made.
(Michael John Hayward, solicitor)

The race to complete: on auction day

After the excitement of the auction and the property contracts exchange, it's easy to think you have time to sit back
and relax. This is absolutely not the case. Once contracts
have been exchanged the race is now on to ensure the property completes in time. On most auction properties there will
be a deadline to complete the sale usually between fourteen
and twenty-eight days. This time passes in the blink of an
eye and so careful organisation, attention to detail and a
whole lot of assertive reminding is required to ensure completion success. There are a huge raft of people who need to
be contacted and informed of the successful purchase – and

who will also need to put wheels in motion to ensure the sale completes in time. On the day of the auction, having bought the property, there are three key things do:

1. **Instruct a solicitor.** In the UK a solicitor is required to complete the legal transaction of a property. If you have used the services of a solicitor to check the property details prior to auction, it is advisable to continue with the same solicitor since much of the initial legal work will have already been completed. If you are arranging finance, it is prudent to inform the solicitor of key people who may need to be contacted to ensure the sale completes on time. The solicitor will need the Memorandum of Contract which was completed at the auction and this should be provided immediately. If you do not have a solicitor, then you will need to find one – and fast. It is sensible to check before instruction that the solicitor you are considering is familiar with property auction purchases and has the time available to ensure the completion deadline is met.

2. **Arrange insurance.** Once contracts have been exchanged, the property will now become your liability. It is essential that adequate insurance is organised swiftly to ensure the property is covered. Insurance should usually take effect from the date of exchange of contracts. If the property is leasehold it is worth checking the details of the lease to ensure the landlord has adequate cover for the property you have purchased. If in doubt, place the property on cover until you have further information.

3. **Inform the finance house.** If finance is being obtained for a property purchase, the lender will need to know

immediately that finance will be required. The lender or broker should be informed of the successful purchase, the completion date and the details of the solicitor you are using. If a survey is required the lender will require the contact details for organising access (this should be checked with the auction house).

LEGAL TIP

Buyers need to make sure they contact their solicitor as soon as they have bought a property at auction and have given their solicitor all the required information as a matter of extreme urgency. The solicitor has limited time to act within the required deadline stipulated in the sale contract and buyers need to appreciate that, if they fail to meet the contractual deadline, they risk losing their deposit money if the seller withdraws. (Michael John Hayward, solicitor)

After the auction . . . a frantic few days

The days following a successful auction purchase are frantic. There are many people to call and chase about the sale, pieces of paper that need signing and returning and decisions to be made very quickly. In addition to the mayhem that will ensue, you will also need to be planning the steps for *after* the sale completion date. This is the time to get everything in order for the next steps. Careful planning and organisation can make or break the success of a project and as the clock is now ticking it's important to ensure you maximise the time you have available between the exchange and completion date.

- **Revisit the property.** Where possible it is advisable to visit the property again after exchange. This will give you the opportunity to double check ideas, gain additional quotes and finalise plans for any works to the property. If the property is tenanted, it is a good idea to introduce yourself as the new owner and arrange a friendly meeting to ensure the tenants are aware of the situation. Any tenants will need to be informed of the future change in rental payments and whom to contact over property management and maintenance issues. It is important to address any concerns they may have and start the relationship on an open and honest footing.

- **Finalise quotes.** It is preferable when revisiting the property for your chosen builder to accompany you to ensure all previously discussed works have been quoted for. The builder needs to have a clear idea of what is involved and book the time into the schedule as necessary. There is nothing worse than accepting a builder's quote, only to find out he no longer has availability to undertake the works. All schedules need to be agreed and a start date planned.

- **Plan your cash flow.** If the property requires refurbishment works the flow of money out of your account will be relentless. Undertaking a renovation requires access to large sums of money to pay for builders, materials and services. It is important to understand the critical points at which big bills will need to be paid and ensure you have made the necessary financial arrangements.

- **Contact the agents.** Unless the renovation is planned to take more than two months to complete, now is a good time to organise for agents (letting and estate agents) to visit the property. This is a great way for you to start networking with potential agents who may market your house and also you will soon get a feel for the agents you prefer. It is preferable to build early engagement with agents and listen to their ideas and opinions about maximising the value of the property and its market appeal.

- **Assert your ownership.** On the day of completion it is important to take accurate meter readings (supported by photographic proof) of the utility meters at the property and inform the suppliers of your new details. This will ensure you are only billed for the usage from the time of your ownership. If the property requires major works, you should contact the council tax department to see if there are any exemptions you can apply for. It is best practice to change all locks on the property as you never know how many keys are in circulation.

What happens if I am delayed or can't complete?

Unfortunately, even with the best will in the world, sometimes delays occur when completing on the purchase of an auction property. These delays are costly, stressful and time-consuming. Generally, the sale contract will set out a penalty interest rate which the buyer must pay to the seller by way of compensation for every day which passes beyond the contractual completion date. Also, if the buyer fails to complete on time, the seller's solicitors will be entitled to serve a 'notice to complete' upon the buyer (or buyer's solicitors) making time of the essence under the contract. Once the notice to complete has been served, the buyer normally has ten working days to complete the matter.

In the event that the sale is not just delayed but in fact can no longer be completed, is where matters get serious, and seriously expensive. If you renege on the contract the vendor is entitled to keep your deposit in full and resell the property. Given this would have been 10 per cent of the sale price this can lead to a loss of several thousands – if not tens of thousands of pounds. Unfortunately, the situation can get even worse. If the vendor resells the property and the price is for less than the original price you contracted to pay, then the vendor is entitled to take legal action against you for the additional loss. This is a scary situation as not only would you have lost the deposit on the property, you would also be liable for any shortfall which may arise. If the vendor resells the property and the proceeds are more than the original sale price, the vendor gets to keep all of the resale price plus the deposit of the original contract. There's no doubt that failure to complete on an auction property is not an option which should ever be considered lightly: the financial ramifications are tremendous.

LEGAL INSIGHT

If the buyer fails to complete, then the seller has various options available to him which includes:

- Rescinding contract.

- Claiming a deposit and any interest on it.

- Forfeit the deposit and any interest on it.

- Re-sell the lot.

- Claim damages from the buyer.

(Michael John Hayward, solicitor)

CASE STUDY: THE LAST-MINUTE FINANCE FIASCO

Some years ago I decided to bid on a one-bedroom flat in Watford. I had arranged the mortgage finance ahead of the auction. The survey had been conducted and the lender had already issued a mortgage offer. The property had a value of approximately £150,000. I attended the auction and was delighted to buy the property for £115,000. I paid the deposit of £11,500 and the completion date was set for just fourteen days later (it was a repossession). I immediately contacted my solicitor about the successful auction purchase and arranged for all the legal documents to be sent to him. He was quite anxious about the fourteen-day completion deadline, but I assuaged his fears when I informed him the surveyor had already attended the property and I had a mortgage offer in principle. I then got on with the task of marketing the property as I was planning to rent the flat out.

All was progressing well until 72 hours before the sale completion date when my solicitor called me with 'very bad news'. A clause had been found in the lease which meant the mortgage company could no longer lend the finance. For some unknown reason, I had not requested my solicitor to check the legals prior to my purchase and so this issue had not been picked up before bidding at auction. I was shell-shocked. I had already paid the £11,500 deposit for the flat and I knew that if I did not complete I stood to lose the entire deposit and also be sued for any shortfall if the vendor failed to resell at the original price. I could not afford to lose the deposit, let alone be sued for any shortfall. It was one of the most stressful moments of my life as I called all friends and family and asked to borrow money from them immediately until I could sort the situation out. Luckily, with their assistance and a personal bank loan, I managed to raise the funds to complete in time – just.

Are there any get-outs?

The documentation relating to buying property at auction is incredibly comprehensive and very much places the onus on the buyer of the property. Therefore it is the responsibility of the prudent buyer to have carried out the due diligence and checks on a property prior to bidding. In the Common Auction Conditions of Sale the major points are very clear:

- The lot is sold subject to all matters contained or referred in the documents (except financial charges: these the seller must discharge on or before completion) and to such of the following as may affect it, whether they arise before or after the contract date and whether or not they are disclosed by the seller or are apparent from inspection of the lot or from the documents.

- The buyer buys with full knowledge of:
  - The documents whether or not the buyer has read them.
  - The physical condition of the lot and what could reasonably be discovered on inspection of it, whether or not the buyer has inspected it.

- The buyer is not relying on the information contained in the particulars or in any replies to preliminary enquiries but on the buyer's own verification of that information. If any information is not correct any liability of the seller and any remedy of the buyer are excluded to the extent permitted by law.

(RICS: Common Auction Conditions of Sale, Edition 3, August 2009)

The simple fact is that buying property at auction requires a prudent buyer to have undertaken prudent due diligence.

> ### *LEGAL TIP*
>
> Sale contracts in auction sales usually state that it is always the buyer's responsibility to check for himself that the information provided by the seller's agents in the auction catalogue is correct and it is always the buyer's responsibility to carry out his own inspections and surveys about the property being sold. (Michael John Hayward, solicitor)

Unfair contract?

The Unfair Contract Terms Act of 1977 prevents a person inserting unfair terms into an agreement. However, this act does not apply to contracts for the sale of land. This means the applicability of the act is quite limited when it comes to auction contracts and would only be justifiably used in connection with the gross misrepresentation of a property bought at auction.

Auctioneers are believed to have a duty of care to buyers to describe lots accurately and any misleading statements about a property may mean they are criminally liable under the Property Misdescriptions Act, 1991. However, while a duty of care is believed to exist, it is only in the cases where a property has been majorly misrepresented and the particulars very misleading that a case may be put forward to have the contract rescinded. In the majority of cases, the prudence of the buyer is paramount and it appears the auctioneer is often absolved of most responsibility. If you do believe a property has been misdescribed, this should be reported to your solicitor immediately and steps should be sought to resolve the situation. Completion will usually be delayed until a satisfactory conclusion is reached or the contract is cancelled.

LEGAL INSIGHT

Under the general principles of contract law, one party to a contract does have the right to terminate that contract if the other party has seriously breached his or her obligations under that contract. However, in property contracts, virtually all of the obligations under that contract will fall upon the buyer's shoulders. There would have to be something seriously wrong with the property (or there would have to be some serious defect with the documents contained in the auction pack) to warrant the buyer walking away from the deal and terminating the contract. For example, if there had been a fraudulent misrepresentation by the seller (or by the auctioneers on behalf of the seller) regarding the property being sold then, in those circumstances, it might be possible for a buyer to withdraw from the contract. (Michael John Hayward, solicitor)

CASE STUDY: THE MISDESCRIBED PROPERTY

Simon is a regular buyer and has been buying property at auction for almost three decades. Having bought hundreds of properties at auction, Simon is well versed in the auction buying process. When he saw a property listed as a 'two-bedroom garden flat' in his local area he was keen to secure the deal. As an experienced cash buyer who has undertaken many building projects he conducted a 'drive by' on the property and did not attend the viewing internally. From the external look and location of the property, Simon felt able to calculate the valuation of the property and estimate what should be paid at auction.

Simon attended the auction and bought the 'two-bedroom garden flat' for £246,000. Just before sale completion he organised a viewing of the property with his builder to schedule the works which would be required. Upon entering the property he got a shock – there was no kitchen, no bathroom – except a single toilet – and, staggeringly, no walls! Simon, while experienced in undertaking major renovations, felt there was something not right about the property. It did not appear to him to be a 'two-bedroom garden flat' and so he started doing more research.

His next step was to visit the local council offices to research the building further. At first the council could not find any record of the property he had bought. All they had on their system were the other two flats in the building – there was no mention of the ground floor flat he had purchased. Simon had to spend considerable time trying to convince the council of the existence of this property he had purchased. It was only when archived records were retrieved that it was discovered the flat he had bought was actually a commercial training centre. The property was not a residential unit and did not have planning permission to be a two-bedroom garden flat.

Simon contacted the auctioneers immediately and informed them of his findings. He also notified his solicitor of the situation. The auctioneer asked Simon what his preferred outcome would be and Simon requested the contract be cancelled as the property he had bought was not what he thought he was buying. The auctioneer agreed to cancel the contract and returned Simon's deposit and refunded him the legal fees he had incurred.

Outbid at auction

'Going to auction and being outbid is so disappointing. I spend days and weeks making sure the property is right for me and then in just a few minutes at the auction I learn it's not right for me after all – and somebody else buys it!'

(David, property buyer)

Being outbid at auction is disappointing. In fact, it's incredibly frustrating. A lot of time, effort and money has been spent researching and preparing for success at auction. When your bid is not successful it can feel like a real blow. This can lead to the auction blues. This is usual. When a sale doesn't happen, the excitement and vigour and all the action which was required pre-auction ends up in an anticlimax. So much hard work – and for what? The excitement and energy quickly turns to a feeling of apathy and emptiness which generally lasts for a few days. It is natural and normal to be disappointed about an anticipated project which then does not happen. However, the auction blues will soon dissipate – even if it takes somewhat longer for the finances to catch up!

In the depths of the auction blues it can feel difficult to appreciate there will be another property. But there always is. There is always another property to try to buy – and you can hope that next time you will be more successful. It is important not to bid, or try to buy a property just for the sake of it or because you have invested a lot of time, energy and money. The bid limit which you calculated is there for a reason – there is no point paying too much for a property just to own a property. It is useful to remind yourself at this point properties are liabilities as well as assets – paying too much for a property could seriously damage your financial wealth – not to mention your mental health.

Being outbid is also a learning process and after an unsuccessful bid it is useful to sit down and analyse the reasons. On many occasions, the answer is simple: the other party were willing to pay more for the property than you. That does not make their purchase right or wrong; it just means they valued the property differently and were willing to pay a higher price. How people value property is a very personal affair and it will all depend on their reasons for purchase. Not all buyers approach property with the same motivations and this is where there is a variance on the price people are willing to pay.

Nevertheless, it is useful to understand if there was anything amiss in the sums you calculated (for example, renovation costs, end value estimates) that may have led you astray in your thinking. It is important to learn, improve and move on. Unfortunately, you may have incurred some expenses in the process of trying to buy a property at auction. These are part and parcel of the nature of buying at auction and are necessary to ensure future success. Most of these costs will have to be written off; however, it is worth keeping hold of all receipts because the costs can usually be offset against a future successful purchase. Being outbid is a fact of life in auctions. It is important to remain positive and ensure you keep your auction team on side. This means informing anybody who assisted you in the research of the auction property that you appreciated their time and next time you intend to be successful. Preparation for success is key – even if it takes a few more auction lots to get there.

CASE STUDY: WHEN 'MORE THAN ENOUGH' STILL WASN'T ENOUGH TO SECURE THE PROPERTY!

Buying property is an emotional experience – especially when you've decided it could be your dream home. When I happened upon a flat in Bloomsbury being sold at auction by executors I fell head over heels in love. The property was in need of updating, but it was well located and had a great feel to it. I was keen to secure the flat as an investment, but also more importantly, as potentially a place where I could move to in the future.

I undertook all the necessary research on the flat including having a survey, arranging the finance ahead of auction and getting the legals checked. When it came to exploring the price comparisons, the task became a little more difficult. As this was not a straight investment, but also a potential home which I intended to own for a long time, it became more difficult to assess the accurate value of a home as opposed to a property. In this case, I started with the base value of the property as both a capital and rental investment and then added another personal premium to my bid limit – an extra amount which I was prepared to pay to secure the property.

Having spoken with a number of investors prior to auction, I felt confident my bid limit was sufficiently high to be in with a good chance of winning the property. My bid limit was almost 30 per cent above the guide price and I was willing to pay more than local estate agents had valued the flat at. The reason I was prepared to pay more for the flat than its current market value was that in the future I intended to potentially occupy the property as my long-term home. This meant I used different indices to arrive at my bid limit, which included allowing for longer-term capital growth estimates as well as how much money I could afford to pay. When I arrived at the auction room I felt quietly confident that I was willing to pay more than enough to successfully secure the sale of the property. But, alas, what I had not prepared for was an overseas investor who was prepared to pay *whatever* it took to secure the flat. After an emotional bidding war it soon became clear the overseas investor had much more money at his disposal than I had – and was much less bothered about how far over market value he went. Sadly, I had to give up on my dream purchase and walk away without my longed-for flat.

Insider Insight

Always, always have a plan B with finances. Even if you believe the mortgage or commercial lending is in place, anything can happen at the last minute. Knowing what options are available can reduce the stress.

Chapter Overview

This chapter has looked at what happens after bidding at auction. The exchange of contracts has been discussed and strict deadlines of sale completion have been highlighted. It is imperative to act swiftly and inform all concerned parties immediately upon purchase to ensure the sale deadline is met. The time between exchange and completion should be used to finalise plans and organise next steps. Any delays in the sale completion date will incur financial penalties being claimed as compensation in addition to the sales price. Being unable to complete on an auction contract has very serious financial consequences which will result in the loss of your deposit and potential legal action. There are very few cases where buyers are able to rescind the contract. Being outbid at auction is disappointing and can lead to the auction blues, although it is useful to learn from missed bids to improve for next time.

Expert Tip

Circle the sale completion date in your calendar and regularly communicate with all related parties to ensure the deadline is adhered to.

Watch Point

Don't get hung up on a property you were outbid on. Identify why the opportunity was not yours and learn from the process so that you are ready for next time.

CHAPTER 9
Tales From the Auction Room

Property auctions offer a unique buying environment where people can literally win or lose a fortune in a matter of minutes. The auction room offers very real success and disaster to buyers – and can be a roller coaster of a journey. Buying property at auction can be hugely profitable, but it can also have its pitfalls. Due diligence, prudence and courage are the hallmarks of a successful auction buyer.

I hope this selection of auction stories will serve to inspire and caution you.

When popular can be hugely profitable

Tom is a regular auction buyer and has been in the game for decades. He loves the cut and thrust of the property auction room and enjoys buying property. One day Tom attended a viewing at a flat in Kensington. It was a one-bedroom property but had the potential to have two bedrooms. Tom was amazed at how busy the viewing was and counted no fewer than 157 people in attendance. Later that week Tom was at the auction when the Kensington flat was offered for sale.

He had not intended bidding for the flat, but soon found himself the winning bidder at £285,000.

Following the auction he visited some estate agents to double check the value of his purchase and decide if he should rent or sell the property. The decision was made for him. An estate agent he had spoken to had clients who wanted to buy his flat from him immediately. In fact, they wanted to take over the purchase of his flat from him at auction so that they could own the flat even sooner. Tom sold the flat to the estate agents' clients without ever going back to the flat or even completing the sale. The clients took over his exchanged sale and less than twenty-eight days later Tom netted a whopping £300,000 profit for the privilege of putting his hand in the air at a property auction.

The Bargain Bought After Auction

I was looking through the results of a recent auction sale when I spotted a one-bedroom flat in Camberwell, London, which had not sold and had a reserve price of £99k. I was surprised that a flat in such a central location could be so cheap. I noticed it was ex-local authority and not the best looking building on the block – however, I thought it was worth a look. I contacted the auctioneers and arranged to view the property. In the meantime I checked the legals to ensure there were no nasty surprises. At the viewing, I was surprised by how spacious the flat was and noted that it even had a garden. I immediately gave my debit card details to the auctioneer and exchanged on the flat. Completion was set for twenty-eight days later. In the meantime, I contacted estate agents and discovered there would be huge appeal for this flat on the resale market – and in its current condition. I was surprised to hear this, and so, having spent just a few days cleaning and toning down the dark blue paintwork, I put it on the market for sale. Just ten days later the property sold for £145,000.

Buy in haste, repent at leisure

John and Daniel are two successful businessmen and friends. John is a successful property investor with a large property portfolio, while Daniel has just sold his business and has started to invest under John's guidance. Looking through the auction catalogues for inspiration the men noticed that property in Stoke-on-Trent seemed very cheap, and so they decided to pay the auction room a visit that evening. The auction was held in a quality hotel which John and Daniel had both checked into. They were both enjoying their evening out, having dined at the hotel, and were having a few drinks at the hotel bar while watching the auction.

John and Daniel were enthralled by the cheap properties on offer, which were priced far lower than anything they were used to. As they were standing at the bar, a property appeared on the screen which was being offered for sale. It was a very large commercial property with thousands and thousands of square footage – and a paying tenant in one part of the building at £400pcm.

Bidding for the property started at £25,000 and the men could not resist. Before they knew it, they had paid £59,000 for a building in Stoke-on-Trent they had never even seen. The next day John and Daniel visited the property they had bought the previous night at auction. They were to get a very nasty shock. The building was huge – but it was also in a very poor state of repair. The roof was literally peeling off and the entire top floor was covered in pigeon droppings! John and Daniel made enquiries locally and discovered the council had identified the building as requiring works and the new owner would be eligible for some part-funded grant works to bring the property up to standard. The new buyers were excited by this news and could not believe their luck – a cheap property and possibly grant money to refurbish it.

The paying tenant who occupied the ground floor was asked to leave and applications for the works were applied for. In the meantime, tenders were sent to local builders to quote for the works which were required. Due to health and safety issues the top floor was cleared of pigeon droppings at a cost in excess of £1,000. The new owners continued to visit the property they had bought although this was becoming increasingly difficult as they lived over 150 miles away. In time, the quotes were received from the builders and the work was going to cost far more than either John or Daniel had ever envisaged. The building required in excess of £250,000 for the refurbishment. The £59,000 building they had bought blind no longer felt so much of a bargain.

While the building was eligible for grant assistance, a condition of the scheme was that John and Daniel would be required to make a contribution to the works. This contribution was close to £100,000. They quickly realised the building had not been the bargain they thought it was. Just months later they placed the property on the market for sale. Given the poor condition of the building, they were forced to sell at auction and achieved a sales price of just £50,000. After all costs had been totalled, and not including all the time that was spent on the project, John and Daniel estimate they lost over £17,000. It was, they claim, their most expensive night out ever!

The property needing 'full' modernisation

A three-bedroom house in Staffordshire was listed for sale at auction. The property was a repossession and was listed in the auction catalogue as requiring 'full modernisation'. The property had a guide price of £70,000. Equivalent properties in the area were valued around £115,000.

I went to view the property and was surprised by the sight which greeted me. The property had a fully fitted quality oak kitchen, beautiful tiled floors, a white downstairs cloakroom, a spacious lounge with a feature fitted fireplace and well-fitted laminate flooring. To the rear there was a huge good quality conservatory which was a fabulous selling feature. Upstairs, the property had three bedrooms with fitted wardrobes and a white bathroom suite with Jacuzzi bath and power shower. The property was double-glazed throughout and had gas central heating. Looking around the property, it was clear the previous owners had spent a considerable sum on improving the property and it was very unclear where the auctioneers had got the idea that the property needed 'full modernisation'. The property had been fully modernised already.

Auction day came and I was prepared to bid on the property. I knew that I was one of only a handful of people who had actually viewed the property and so I felt pretty confident I didn't have too much competition. But as bidding started I was in for a shock. The auctioneer opened the bidding at £55,000 and within seconds the price had reached £68,000. And then it stopped. There was a hush. Nobody moved. I put my hand in the air. The next bid was £70,000. The auctioneer took my bid. And then there was silence. Nobody bid against me. Nobody even looked up. People were busy foraging in their auction catalogues looking for the next lot. 'Going once,' called the auctioneer. Still nobody moved. 'Going twice,' he called again. My heart was pounding. 'Going for the third and final time . . .' My pulse was racing and my head was spinning – was this really going to happen? The auctioneer banged his gavel down and I bought the fully modernised property for £70,000! The next week I invited estate agents around to the property to value it for sale – all agreed the value was £115,000.

Getting more than you bargained for

Derek's main business is in transport and storage, but as a hobby he likes to dabble in property auctions. As part of his business Derek has a fleet of vans and is always struggling to find enough space to park them all. He was keen to expand to some new areas and had started to look at sites farther from his home territory. Derek was attracted to buying at auction as he was a cash buyer and there seemed to be some interesting sites available at competitive prices. He attended an auction in London and bought a site to be used as storage for some his vans at a location in Essex. Derek paid £120,000 for the site and felt this was a good purchase.

Derek had glanced over the legals before buying the site but had not instructed a solicitor because he had only made a definite decision to bid the night before auction. When his solicitor contacted him he was shocked to discover the site he had bought for his vans was far larger than he had originally anticipated and the catalogue particulars displayed. Derek had actually purchased the site and some garages and a parking area on adjoining land. Derek viewed the additional land he had acquired and felt it was more suited to building houses than for his business. He contacted the planning department, submitted plans and built four houses on the extra land. Derek believes the extra land which he 'accidently acquired' was worth in excess of £200,000 on top of the £120,000 price he paid for the original site at auction.

It's always best to get proper legal advice before you bid

Mr Judd had spotted the house of his dreams and thought it would make an ideal family home for him, his wife and child. He and his wife attended all viewings before the sale date and were excited about bidding for their new home at auction. They managed to secure the property for just under their final bid limit and were keen to start planning the works they were going to do to make it their own home.

Mr and Mrs Judd had organised the finances and obtained quotes for the refurbishment works before auction. As the property was a freehold house, the legal documents appeared to be quite straightforward, and so Mr Judd had looked at the paperwork himself. He had not had the legals checked by a solicitor prior to bidding.

The property was being sold by receivers for a mortgage lender. The receivers, who were selling the property, had actually been appointed by a particular bank but, the bank in question wasn't the first charge holder on the property, but was ranking as a second charge holder on the property. Mr Judd bought the property at auction without checking the sale contract beforehand. Unfortunately, the sale contract said nothing whatsoever about the second charge holder ensuring that the first charge holder's mortgage on the property (i.e. a prior mortgage held by a different lender) would be repaid and cancelled at the Land Registry when the sale was completed.

Mr Judd was buying the property with the assistance of

mortgage finance, and so the solicitor was required to give a 'report on title' to Mr Judd's lender. However, the solicitor was unable to give a clean report on title until written assurances had been received from the seller's solicitors that the previous mortgage registered against the property would be removed and cancelled at the Land Registry once the transaction had been completed. Fortunately for the Judds, the matter was resolved satisfactorily in due course. However, it did cause significant delays in completing the transaction and Mr Judd was required to pay considerable late interest penalties to the seller for failing to complete the transaction on the required date.

Offering before auction is not always the best choice

James had seen a flat in London he liked very much. The flat was located in a good part of town and in an ex-local authority block built in the 1920s. He felt the area had good vibes and, while the flat was dated, it appeared to be an easy property for him to refurbish cheaply and quickly. He attended the viewing and was concerned by the number of people who also seemed interested in the flat – it suggested to him there would be a lot of competition in the room and he was unsure of his chances of success.

The flat had a guide price of £125,000, but James estimated the end value to be roughly £170,000. As he liked the flat and the area so much he decided to offer on the flat before auction. He offered a price of £142,000 to secure the property before auction. The vendors rejected his offer, preferring for the property to be sold in the room. On auction day James braced himself for disappointment. His maximum bid was £142,000 and, as the vendors had already rejected his offer before auction, he was sure they expected it to sell for more in the room.

The bidding started slowly on the flat and James felt encouraged that he may be in with a chance. The bidding seemed to have become very slow and so he put in a bid at £125,000. And then he waited. The room didn't seem to react at all. James was very confused – the auctioneer had started the final calling of the property. Was he definitely the final bidder at £125,000? The auctioneer looked directly at James. The hammer had fallen – the flat was his. At just £125,000 he bought the flat at auction – £17,000 less than he had offered to buy it for before auction.

The chapel that was 'illegal' to live in

Adam is a seasoned auction buyer and especially loves buying in December when he believes most people are preoccupied with the impending Christmas holidays. The week before Christmas, Adam was at a property auction in London. He had marked several properties of interest in his catalogue but so far the bidding had gone far in excess of his set limits. He was feeling quite disheartened about his chances of bagging a bargain when he spotted a chapel which would be going up for sale in a few lots' time. The chapel was located in Cambridgeshire, an area that Adam knew quite well.

When the bidding for the chapel started, Adam watched with interest as the bidding slowed around the £55,000 mark. He knew the chapel would be worth far more than that and so started bidding. He had not read the legal pack, nor even seen the property, but he felt sure the property was a bargain not to be missed. Adam won the bidding at £61,000. He was elated to have bought a chapel in Cambridgeshire at such a cheap price.

Straight after the auction he called his solicitor to inform him of his new purchase and contacted the local agent who was dealing with the property. He organised a visit to the property the next day to view his new purchase.

When Adam arrived at the chapel he was delighted to see the property was in good condition. It was a repossession that required some updating, but he could see it had good potential and an opportunity to make some money. He set about drawing up schedules of work and talking with local estate agents to calculate the best way to extract maximum value from the project.

A few days after the auction Adam's solicitor called him to enquire about the existence of a cottage close to the chapel. Adam was perplexed: he had noticed there was a derelict cottage located quite close to the rear of the chapel but had not paid it much attention. His solicitor then informed him that the chapel and the cottage were actually interrelated with regards the planning conditions for the chapel; the chapel had only been granted the status and use of a residential dwelling as long as the cottage was not used as a residential dwelling. This caused much confusion as both the chapel and the cottage were on different titles and owned by different people. At first, Adam did not consider this to be an issue as the cottage in question was derelict and not suitable for habitation, while the chapel had recently been lived in until the bank had taken ownership.

However, the major issue this planning condition posed was about the proposed refurbishment Adam planned for the chapel. While the cottage was derelict, if the owner suddenly appeared and wanted to live in the cottage as a dwelling that would then render the chapel an illegal residential dwelling. Adam submitted plans to the council to try to separate the planning conditions of the cottage and the chapel, but the council were adamant the two properties were interlinked – even though they were owned by different people. Adam also tried to track down the owner of the cottage, but he could not trace them as the registered address of the owners was the derelict cottage.

One year later Adam admitted defeat. He realised the issues with the chapel were going to take a very long time to resolve (if they ever could be) and, as such, any major renovation expenditure incurred would be a mistake if the property had the possibility of being classified as an 'illegal' residential dwelling. Given the issues with the chapel the only option he had was to sell it again through auction – it sold for £75,000.

The Scarborough flat with a sting . . . and a win

David has been buying property from auction for over twenty-five years and is a regular face in the room. He prefers to buy in London and the south-east – but when he spots a bargain he is not bothered where it is located.

At auction one day David saw a one-bedroom flat in Scarborough about to be sold. The flat was situated in a handsome period building and David decided the bid price of £35,000 sounded a good buy – he was prepared to bid £500 more than the current bidder. He put his hand in the air. His first bid of £500 more on the Scarborough flat became the final bid and David won the property at £35,500.

After the auction David requested the legal papers to check through and to send to his solicitor. He was surprised to see that as the buyer he was also liable for all the seller's costs including all auction fees, legal fees, marketing costs and so on. He had not seen a clause like this before, but he had now bought the flat and it was too late to query them. He discovered the seller's costs totalled just over £4,000.

David started contacting local estate agents in Scarborough to obtain resale estimates for the flat. As it happened, he came across the local estate agents who had been marketing the property for sale before it was entered for auction. He discovered prior to auction the estate agents had interest in the flat and they believed a marketing price of £55,000 could be achievable. David was due to complete the sale in just a few days' time and he made arrangements with the local estate agents to market the property for him.

Three weeks after the property had been marketed for sale with the estate agents, David accepted a cash offer of £51,000 for the flat with the sale completing just four weeks later. In just seven weeks David had bought and sold the flat without ever viewing it or visiting the area and pocketed a profit of over £10,000!

CHAPTER 10
Simple Steps to Auction Success

Buying property at auction can seem like hard work, but in reality much of the process is simpler than buying private treaty. The fact is, when buying property at auction you get to know a property's entire story all at once – and it is this that can seem overwhelming.

Most of us are used to the private treaty method of buying property, which is where information is drip-fed to us over a protracted period of time. At auction, this same information is available but the difference is that it is available all at once. Moreover, the information needs to be checked and understood before committing to buy.

Buying property at auction does require work beforehand, but if you follow this auction success checklist you will see how straightforward the process is:

1. Get the auction catalogue and find a property of interest.
2. Check the location of the property on Google Maps.

3. Read the basic legals and ask: 'Why is this property being sold at auction?'
4. View the property (use the property survey checklist on pages 72 to 74).
5. Research the current value and end value of the property.
6. Estimate the costs and time frame of the project.
7. Get the legal pack checked, the property surveyed and the finance arranged.
8. Calculate the bid price and set your upper limit.
9. Attend the auction room, or register to bid.
10. Bid and win!

Throughout the guide, I have provided you with an abundance of key tips, insights and watch points. The auction journey involves a lot of work and things to remember, so I have simplified this into a comprehensive Auction Tip Journey.

So here's to taking the first step in your new property adventure!

At the start of your auction adventure, remember:
- Auctions are well known for the variety of properties they sell, but you can also find more typical homes being sold at auction.

- Do not assume auction property is always cheap, or cheaper than estate agents, just because it is being sold at auction.

- Auction properties can, at times, sell for more than the market value due to the excitement and buzz of the auction room.

- Auction property sales complete faster than private

treaty sales, however, preparation and planning can make this possible within the timeframe.

- Auctions are the most transparent way to buy property – all of the information is available upfront so you know what you're buying.

- Many companies and organisations have to sell at auction to show they achieved market value for a property.

- Set up property website search alerts to keep you updated with properties in your area.

- Watch out for 'mismatched' properties in an auction catalogue as they can offer some of the best bargains.

When you've found a property you like:

- Auction houses take great care to prepare accurate property details – but thorough research is always required before buying a property.

- If it's the first lot in the auction catalogue, be prepared to spend considerably more than the guide price if you want to be in with a chance of success.

- The volume of properties and tight deadlines auction houses deal with can often mean critical information may not be received until very close to the auction sale day.

- Many people still think 'you can't go wrong with property' and buy properties from the catalogue on the basis of the photograph and particulars. Appearances can be deceptive – always view a property internally before buying.

When you're ready to view:

- Arrive early at a property viewing to survey the outside of the property and check any external issues thoroughly on the internal viewing.

- Take along a copy of the title plan and check what you're buying is what you're buying!

- Never listen to what other viewers say on viewings – do your own research and don't listen to hearsay.

- Don't be put off by a popular property viewing – it does not always mean high prices at auction.

You must be a detective:

- Properties sold at auction may have limited scope for asking further legal questions – especially if the vendor has never lived at the property (for example, repossession sale).

- Properties are sold at auction for a number of reasons, so thorough research is required to understand the potential issues which may be in store.

- It's a good rule of thumb to be extra vigilant when buying property at auction and always ask: 'Why didn't this sell through an estate agent?'

- Talk to the neighbours – find out what they know about the property and any issues they've seen or heard about.

- Always look for something which is out of place and keep asking 'why?'.

- If a property sounds too good to be true, it usually is. The onus is on you to know what you're buying: dig deeper and deeper and ask yet more questions.

When you're seriously interested and considering to bid:

- Preparing to buy a property at auction requires professional expertise in many areas. It is advisable to build a 'dream team' of trusted experts to call upon when looking to purchase property at auction.

- The special conditions are key documents to read – make sure you know the 'naughties' before you bid and buy.

- The practice of demanding a contribution towards the vendor's costs of selling at auction is increasing. These costs can add up to thousands of pounds.

- Gain maximum value by instructing a survey early.

- If buying leasehold and there is less than eighty years left on the lease, it could prove expensive to extend. Make sure you have three years' service charge accounts to assess the property's running costs.

- Always have a solicitor read through the legals – if anything is missing be cautious and only act under expert supervision. Occasionally, documents may be missing on purpose – a good solicitor is well versed in these matters.

- Most solicitors will carry out a pre-auction check before you buy for a minimal cost – legal issues can cost far more to resolve than any refurbishment budget, plus adverse legals can prevent funding.

- Ensure you understand all of the contractual and legal conditions which relate to buying property at auction. If in doubt – ask!

If you need to raise finance, remember:

- A kitchen sink and toilet are prerequisites to obtaining mortgage finance.

- If the seller has owned the property for less than six months you'll struggle to finance it.

- Funding must always be sorted out prior to bidding at auction – the paperwork process can take a long time.

- The need to raise speedy finance can be a barrier to auction purchase, but with preparation and organisation it can be done – plus some vendors are starting to allow six-week completion dates.

- Always, always have a plan B with regards to finance. You can never plan too much when it comes to finding finance to buy property at auction.

You need to know how much the property is worth:

- An asking price for a property is not the same as the sold price for a property.

- Online valuation tools and assessing comparable properties will provide you with a valuation range of the property.

- Always bear in mind the ceiling price of a property, these ceilings are very hard to smash no matter how great the finish.

- Money is made when you buy, not when you sell. Buy a property at a good price and you will always make money.

How to add value and calculate costs:

- Be cost effective in refurbishment works. It is very easy to try to fix everything but this is not always required; add value in areas which are valued.

- As a general guide, the value added to a property should be at least double the cost of the works.

- A project should not be undertaken for less than a 10 per cent profit margin.

- Treat writing a schedule of works like writing a shopping list: it is a list of all the works you want to buy!

- Be cautious of any quote which is very low and ensure you understand what is and is not included.

- Buying property at auction involves taking risks. All risks should be quantified against the rewards potentially gained.

- Calculate what an opportunity is worth to you, but remember the numbers do not lie – if a deal does not stack up, walk away.

When auction sale day arrives:

- It is always best to bid from the auction room, so where possible try to attend the sale day.

- If you can't make it to the room, proxy bids and telephone bids are designed to work on the same basis as if you were in the room and should not disadvantage buyers.

- If you're planning to buy with someone else and bid on their behalf (for example, a joint purchase) make sure you take their ID and details with you.

- Arrive early to check any amendments and survey the room. Calculate the approximate time your bid should be sold and prepare to succeed!

- Last-minute changes to auction particulars can have a serious impact on the value of the property you are planning to bid on. Any amendments should be checked thoroughly before bidding.

- Never be late to bid – it's well known for people to arrive late and miss their lot.

- If your bid limit ends in a 0 or a 5 try to add one more bid to make the limit more uneven, for example, £66,000/£71,000.

- Write down your upper limit to ensure you focus once the auction starts.

- Treat the auction sale day as a 'day out'. Bidding will be over in minutes so organise to meet friends later to celebrate or commiserate!

In the auction room, remember:

- Auction sale day is about creating an environment and an atmosphere where people want to buy – auctioneers love auctioneering!

- The auctioneer wants to get the best sale price for the vendor when he bangs the gavel down.

- It is very easy to get caught up in the excitement of auction and so it is important to keep a clear head and your guard up.

- Many property auctioneers can appear intimidating when stood high on the rostrum – but remember they need you, the buyer, to help them do their job.

- Never be afraid to change your mind before bidding. If a property does not feel right do not be pressurised to buy.

When the bidding gets started:

- Stand at the back, survey the room and the competition – you'll be able to pick up when you need to come in.

- Do not get carried away. Have an upper limit and stick to it.

- Never be afraid to request a different bid increment – the worst thing that can happen is the auctioneer will say no.

- You can never know somebody else's psyche – but changing the bid increments can disrupt the flow of the room and the rhythm of the bidding.

- Regular auction buyers will only buy at the limits they set. They profit from property and remain financially focussed.

- A good auctioneer will be able to create the illusion of bidding – whether or not there is any in the room – and he will not let on if he is taking 'bids off the wall'.

- Most properties have a reserve price, below which they cannot be sold. Auctioneers help bidders to reach the reserve and should never feel hard done by.

When you've successfully bid and won:

- Always give full and proper particulars of all the people who intend to purchase the property.

- Make sure you inform your solicitor and finance house and send the paperwork as soon as possible.

- Circle the completion date in your calendar and meet the deadline.

If you're buying after auction:
- If buying unsold property after auction, it is a race to exchange – the first to exchange wins.

- Auction conditions still prevail with property bought after auction.

If you got outbid:
- Don't get hung up on a property you were outbid on. Identify why the opportunity was not yours and learn from the process so you are ready for next time.

If you can't complete:
- If you fail to complete an auction purchase it's a serious matter. You can kiss goodbye to your deposit and cross your fingers it sells for more than you bid, otherwise you'll be liable for the shortfall.

- Getting out of an auction contract is nigh on impossible. There has to be a serious breach of contract or something seriously wrong with the documents to warrant the buyer walking away from the deal and terminating the contract.

Buying property at auction is scarily exciting – but also very, very addictive! Once you get the hang of it, I doubt you'll ever go back to an estate agent again.

Good luck and I look forward to seeing you soon in the auction room!

Appendix

Auctioneer directory

Auction houses are located all over the country and come in various shapes and sizes. The directory below contains the most active residential and commercial auction houses in the UK and Ireland. Auction houses have been listed according to region, however some – especially those based in London – will offer properties all over the country.

Eigroup.co.uk have kindly supplied all data for the auctioneer directory.

East Anglia

Aldreds
t. 01493 853853
http://www.aldreds.co.uk

Arnolds Keys
t. 01603 620551
http://www.arnolds.uk.com

Auction House East Anglia
t. 01603 505100
http://www.auctionhouse.uk.net/eastanglia/default.aspx

Brown & Co.
t. 01603 629871
http://www.brown-co.com

Cheffins
t. 01223 213777
http://www.cheffins.co.uk

Clarke & Simpson
t. 01728 724200
http://www.clarkeandsimpson.co.uk

Durrants
t. 01502 713490
http://www.durrants.com

Goldings
t. 01473 210200
http://www.goldingsauctions.co.uk

TW Gaze
t. 01379 641341
http://www.twgaze.com

William H. Brown (Norwich)
t. 01603 598975
http://www.williamhbrownauctions-norwich.co.uk

East Midlands

Auction House Leicestershire
t. 0116 2855566
http://www.auctionhouse.uk.net/leicestershire/default.aspx

Auction House N. Lincs, N. Notts & South Yorkshire
t. 01427 616436
http://www.auctionhouse.uk.net/northlincs

Auction House Richard Greener
t. 01604 230222
http://www.auctionhouse.uk.net/richardgreener/default.aspx

Auction House South Lincolnshire & East Leicestershire
t. 01476 591900
http://www.auctionhouse.uk.net/southlincsandeastleics

Bagshaws Ashbourne
t. 01335 342201
http://www.bagshaws.com

Bagshaws Bakewell
t. 01629 812777
http://www.bagshaws.com

Bagshaws Residential
t. 01332 542298
http://www.bagshawsauctions.co.uk

Barnes
t. 01623 554084
http://www.wabarnes.co.uk

Copelands
t. 01246 232698
http://www.copelands-uk.co.uk

East Midland Property Auction – I AM Sold
t. 0845 5193126
http://www.iam-sold.co.uk

Fidler Taylor
t. 01629 580228
http://www.fidler-taylor.co.uk

Graham Penny (Derby)
t. 01332 242880
http://www.grahampenny.com

Graham Penny (Nottingham)
t. 01159 588702
http://www.grahampenny.com

HEB Chartered Surveyors
t. 0115 950 6611
http://www.heb.co.uk

Savills (Nottingham)
t. 0115 934 8000
http://auctions.savills.co.uk

Shonki Brothers (London Road)
t. 0116 254 3373
http://www.shonkibrothers.com

Shonki Brothers (Narborough Road)
t. 0116 255 7573
http://www.shonkibros.com

Shouler & Son
t. 01664 560181
http://www.shoulers.co.uk

Swindells Auctioneers
t. 01522 789191
http://www.swindellsauctioneers.co.uk

The County Property Auction
t. 01522 504360
http://www.jhwalter.co.uk/propertyauctions

Wallace Jones
t. 0115 946 8946
http://www.wallacejones.net

London

Acuitus
t. 020 7034 4850
http://www.acuitus.co.uk

Allsop Commercial
t. 020 7437 6977
http://www.allsop.co.uk

Allsop Residential
t. 020 7494 3686
http://www.allsop.co.uk

Andrew Scott Robertson
t. 020 7703 4401
http://www.as-r.co.uk

Athawes Son & Co.
t. 020 8992 0056
http://www.athawesauctioneers.co.uk

Auction House London
t. 020 7625 9007
http://www.auctionhouselondon.co.uk

Barnard Marcus
t. 020 8741 9990
http://www.barnardmarcusauctions.co.uk

Barnett Ross
t. 020 8492 9449
http://www.barnettross.co.uk

Brendons Auctioneers
t. 08456 525251
http://www.brendonsauctioneers.co.uk

CBRE
t. 020 7182 2000
http://www.cbreauctions.com

Drivers & Norris
t. 020 7607 5001
http://www.drivers.co.uk

Eddisons London
t. 020 7484 8317
http://www.eddisons.com

Harman Healy
t. 020 8649 7255
http://www.harman-healy.co.uk

Lambert Smith Hampton
t. 020 7198 2280
http://www.lshauctions.com

London and Country Property Auctions
t. 020 7908 1305
http://www.londonandcountrypropertyauctions.com

McHugh & Co.
t. 020 7485 0112
http://www.mchughandco.com

Mustbesold.com
t. 01332 290958
http://www.mustbesold.com

Savills (London – National)
t. 020 7824 9091
http://auctions.savills.co.uk

Strettons
t. 020 8520 8383
http://www.strettons.co.uk

North-East

Auction House North East
t. 0845 4597000
http://www.auctionhouse.uk.net/northeast/default.aspx

Auction House Tees Valley
t. 0845 2412112
http://www.auctionhouse.uk.net/teesvalley/default.aspx

Great North Property Auction – I AM Sold
t. 0845 5193126
http://www.iam-sold.co.uk

Pattinson Property Auctions
t. 08451 461582
http://www.pattinson.co.uk

The Agents Property Auction
t. 01661 831360
http://www.agentspropertyauction.com

North-West

Allitt Auctioneers
t. 01253 294596
http://www.allitt.co.uk/auction.php

Andrew Kelly Auctions
t. 01706 767030
http://www.andrew-kelly.co.uk

Auction House Cheshire & North East Wales
t. 08444 180268
http://www.auctionhouse.uk.net/cheshireandnortheastwales/default.aspx

Auction House Cumbria
t. 0845 8725452
http://www.auctionhouse.uk.net/cumbria/default.aspx

Auction House Huddersfield & Halifax
t. 08444 140929
http://www.auctionhouse.uk.net/huddersfieldandhalifax/default.aspx

Auction House Lancashire
t. 0845 3105700
http://www.auctionhouse.uk.net/lancashire/default.aspx

Auction House Manchester
t. 08444 140929
http://www.auctionhouse.uk.net/manchester

Auction House Smith & Sons
t. 0151 647 9272
http://www.smithandsons.net

Cumbrian Properties – The Agents Property Auction
t. 01661 831360
http://www.agentspropertyauction.com

Eddisons Manchester
t. 0161 831 9444
http://www.eddisons.com

Edward Mellor Auctions
t. 0161 443 4740
http://www.edwardmellor.co.uk

Fisher German Denton Clark
t. 01244 409660
http://www.dentonclark.co.uk

Meller Braggins
t. 01565 632618
http://www.mellerbraggins.com

Metcalf's
t. 01253 624047
http://www.metcalfestateagents.co.uk

Michael C.L. Hodgson
t. 01539 721375
http://www.michael-cl-hodgson.co.uk

Miller Metcalfe
t. 01204 535353
http://www.mmauction.co.uk

Pugh
t. 08442 722444
http://www.pugh-company.co.uk

Roger Hannah Auctions
t. 0161 817 3399
http://www.rogerhannahauctions.co.uk

Sutton Kersh Auctions
t. 0151 207 6315
http://www.suttonkersh.co.uk

The Auction People
t. 08442 722444
http://www.pugh-company.co.uk

Venmore Auctions
t. 0151 236 6746
http://www.venmoreauctions.co.uk

Wright Manley Chester
t. 01244 317833
http://www.wrightmanley.co.uk

Wright Manley Tarporley
t. 01829 731300
http://www.wrightmanley.co.uk

North-West Home Counties

Auction House Beds & Bucks
t. 01234 351000
http://www.auctionhouse.uk.net/bedsandbucks/default.aspx

Auction House East Herts & West Essex
t. 0800 0126714
http://www.auctionhouse.uk.net/easthertsandwestessex/default.aspx

Fisher German Banbury
t. 01295 271555
http://www.fishergerman.co.uk

Martin & Pole
t. 01189 780777
http://www.martinpole.co.uk

Network Auctions
t. 020 7871 0420
http://www.networkauctions.co.uk

Romans
t. 0800 0939994
http://www.romans.co.uk/auctions

Salter McGuinness
t. 020 8907 1222
http://www.saltermcguinness.co.uk

SM Properties
t. 01296 623051
http://www.charrisonproperties.co.uk

Tayler & Fletcher Chipping Norton
t. 01608 644344
http://www.taylerandfletcher.co.uk

Thompson Wilson Estate Agents and Auctioneers
t. 01494 474234
http://www.thompsonwilson.co.uk

South-East Home Counties

Austin Gray
t. 01273 201980
http://www.austingray.co.uk

Clive Emson
t. 01622 608400
http://www.cliveemson.co.uk

Countrywide Property Auctions
t. 01245 344133
http://www.countrywidepropertyauctions.co.uk

Dedman Gray
t. 01702 311010
http://www.dedmanauctions.com

Fox & Sons (Southampton)
t. 023 8033 8066
http://www.foxandsonsauctions.co.uk

Hair & Son
t. 01702 432255
http://www.hairandson.co.uk

Hobbs Parker
t. 01233 502222
http://www.hobbsparker.co.uk

Ibbett Mosely
t. 01732 456731
http://www.ibbettmosely.co.uk/home

Nesbits
t. 023 9286 4321
http://www.nesbits.co.uk

Parsons Son & Basley
t. 01273 326171
http://www.psandb.co.uk

Pearsons
t. 023 8047 4274
http://www.pearsons.com

South-West

Auction House Devon & Cornwall
t. 01837 52381
http://www.auctionhouse.uk.net/devonandcornwall

Auction House West of England
t. 0117 946 4949
http://www.auctionhouse.uk.net/westofengland

Besley Hill
t. 0117 970 1551
http://www.besleyhillsurveyit.co.uk

Bradleys
t. 01395 223336
http://www.bradleys-auctions.tv

Carter Jonas – Wells
t. 01749 677667
http://www.carterjonas.co.uk

Clive Emson
t. 0845 8500333
http://www.cliveemson.co.uk

Cooper & Tanner
t. 01373 455060
http://www.cooperandtanner.co.uk

Greenslade Taylor Hunt
t. 01278 425555
http://www.gth.net

Hollis Morgan
t. 0117 973 6565
http://www.hollismorgan.co.uk

Kivells Launceston
t. 01566 777777
http://www.kivells.co.uk

Maggs & Allen
t. 0117 949 1888
http://www.maggsandallen.co.uk

Miller & Son
t. 01326 311666
http://www.millerson.com

Phillips Smith & Dunn Barnstaple
t. 01271 327878
http://www.phillipsland.com

Shobrook & Co. Ltd
t. 01752 663341
http://www.shobrook.co.uk

Stags Exeter
t. 01392 255202
http://www.stags.co.uk

Stephen & Co.
t. 01934 621101
http://www.stephenand.co.uk

Strakers
t. 01380 727105
http://www.strakers.co.uk/next-auction.ashx

Symonds & Sampson
t. 01258 473766
http://www.symondsandsampson.co.uk

Tayler & Fletcher
t. 01451 820913
http://www.taylerandfletcher.co.uk

The Auction Agents Devon
t. 01392 349111
http://www.theauctionagents.com

Westcountry Property Auctions
t. 0870 2414 343
http://www.westcountrypropertyauctions.co.uk

West Midlands

Andrew Grant
t. 01905 734735
http://www.andrew-grant.co.uk

Auction House Birmingham & the Black Country
t. 01922 615222
http://www.auctionhouse.uk.net/birmingham

Auction House Coventry & Warwickshire
t. 02476 374949
http://www.auctionhouse.uk.net/hawkins/default.aspx

Bagshaws Uttoxeter
t. 01889 562811
http://www.bagshaws.com

Boot & Son
t. 01543 505454
http://www.bootandson.co.uk

Bowen Son & Watson
t. 01691 622534
http://www.bowensonandwatson.co.uk

Bury & Hilton
t. 01538 383344
http://www.buryandhilton.co.uk

Butters John Bee
t. 01782 211180
http://www.buttersjohnbee.com

Cottons
t. 0121 247 2233
http://www.cottonsproperty.co.uk

CP Bigwood
t. 0121 233 5046
http://www.bigwood.uk.com

Derek Spires & Co.
t. 0121 420 4646
http://www.derekspiresandco.com

G. Herbert Banks
t. 01299 896968
http://www.gherbertbanks.co.uk

Graham Watkins & Co.
t. 01538 373308
http://www.grahamwatkins.co.uk

Griffiths & Charles
t. 01905 726464
http://www.griffiths-charles.co.uk

Halls
t. 01743 284777
http://www.hallsgb.com

Howkins & Harrison
t. 01788 564680
http://www.howkinsandharrison.co.uk

John Amos & Company
t. 01568 610310
http://www.johnamos.co.uk

John Earle & Son
t. 01564 794343
http://www.johnearle.co.uk

John Goodwin
t. 01531 634648
http://www.johngoodwin.co.uk

John Shepherd Chartered Surveyors
t. 01564 783866
http://www.johnshepherd.com

K. Stuart Swash
t. 01902 710626
http://www.kstuartswash.co.uk

Louis Taylor
t. 01782 260222
http://www.louis-taylor.co.uk

Loveitts
t. 02476 527789
http://www.loveitts.co.uk

McCartneys
t. 01497 820778
http://www.mccartneys.co.uk

Pennycuick Collins
t. 0121 665 4163
http://www.pennycuick.co.uk

Phipps & Pritchard
t. 01562 822244
http://www.phippsandpritchard.co.uk

Pughs
t. 01531 631122
http://www.hjpugh.co.uk

R.G. & R.B. Williams
t. 01989 567233
http://www.rgandrbwilliams.co.uk

Sunderlands & Thompsons
t. 01432 278888
http://www.st-hereford.co.uk

The Auction Agents
t. 0121 647 6990
http://www.theauctionagents.com

Whittaker & Biggs
t. 01538 372006
http://www.whittakerandbiggs.co.uk

Yorkshire and the Humber

Auction House Blundells
t. 0114 223 0777
http://www.blundells.com

Auction House Hull & East Yorkshire
t. 01377 241919
http://www.auctionhouse.uk.net/hullandeastyorkshire

Auction House Stephenson & Son
t. 01904 486700
http://www.auctionhouse.uk.net/stephensonandson

Auction House West Yorkshire
t. 0113 393 3482
http://www.auctionhouse.uk.net/westyorkshire/default.aspx

Boultons
t. 01484 515029
http://www.boultonsauctions.co.uk

Bramleys
t. 01484 530361
http://www.bramleys.com

East Yorkshire Property Auction – I AM Sold
t. 0845 5193 126
http://www.iam-sold.co.uk

Eddisons Leeds
t. 0113 209 1099
http://www.eddisons.com

Feather Smailes & Scales
t. 01423 534183
http://www.fssproperty.co.uk

Hunters Property Auctions
t. 01904 621026
http://www.yorkshirepropertyauctions.co.uk

Mark Jenkinson & Son
t. 0114 276 0151
http://www.markjenkinson.co.uk

Northern Lincolnshire Property Auction – I AM Sold
t. 0845 5193 126
http://www.iam-sold.co.uk

Regional Property Auctioneers
t. 01302 304432
http://www.barnsdales.co.uk

Robin Jessop
t. 01677 425950
http://www.robinjessop.co.uk

Sharpes
t. 01274 731217
http://www.sharpes-estate-agents.co.uk

Walker Singleton
t. 01484 477600
http://www.walkersingleton.co.uk

West Yorkshire Property Auction – I AM Sold
t. 0845 5193 126
http://www.iam-sold.co.uk

Wilbys Chartered Surveyors
t. 01226 299221
http://www.wilbys.net

William H. Brown (Leeds)
t. 01302 710490
http://www.williamhbrownauctions-leeds.co.uk

Wm Sykes & Son
t. 01484 683543
http://www.wmsykes.co.uk

Northern Ireland

BRG Gibson
t. 028 9039 3966
http://www.brggibsonauctions.com

Osborne King
t. 028 9027 0000
http://www.osborneking.com

Wilsons (Northern Ireland)
t. 028 9034 2626
http://www.wilsonsauctions.com

Scotland

SVA Property Auctions Ltd
t. 0131 624 6640
http://www.sva-auctions.co.uk

Wilsons (Scotland)
t. 01294 833444
http://www.wilsonsauctions.com

Wales

All Wales Auction – North Wales Auction
t. 0800 905 905
http://www.allwalesauction.com

Astleys
t. 01792 655891
http://www.astleysamuelleeder.co.uk

Auction House South East Wales
t. 01633 212555
http://www.auctionhouse.uk.net/southeastwales

Auction House South West Wales
t. 01437 761457
http://www.auctionhouse.uk.net/southwestwales/default.aspx

Clee Tompkinson Francis
t. 01269 591884
http://www.ctf-uk.com

Clough & Co.
t. 01745 812049
http://www.cloughco.com

Dafydd Hardy Auctions
t. 01248 711999
http://www.dafyddhardy.com

Dawsons
t. 01792 646060
http://www.dawsonsproperty.co.uk

Harry Ray & Company
t. 01938 552555
http://www.harryray.com

Herbert R. Thomas
t. 01446 776379
http://www.hrt.uk.com

John Francis
t. 01267 221554
http://www.johnfrancis.co.uk

Jones Peckover
t. 01745 812127
http://www.jonespeckover.com

Morris Marshall & Poole
t. 01938 554818
http://www.morrismarshall.co.uk

Mustbesold Wales
t. 01685 387320
http://www.mustbesoldwales.com/index.php

Newland Rennie Wilkins Chepstow
t. 01291 626775
http://www.nrwproperty.com

Norman Lloyd & Co. (Llanidloes)
t. 01686 413209
http://www.normanlloyd.com

Paul Fosh Auctions
t. 01633 254044
http://www.paulfoshauctions.com

Seel & Co.
t. 029 2037 0117
http://www.seelandco.com

Ireland

Eddisons Ireland
t. 00353 1 906 0600
http://www.eddisons.com/ireland

Real Estate Alliance
t. 00353 1 669 9996
http://www.realestatealliance.ie

Allsop Space
t. 00353 1 678 9748
http://www.allsopspace.ie

Index